Types
in the
Old
Testament

Types
in the
Old
Testament

ADA R. HABERSHON

KREGEL PUBLICATIONS
Grand Rapids, Michigan 49501

Types in the Old Testament, by Ada R. Habershon.
Published 1988 by Kregel Publications, a division of
Kregel, Inc. All rights reserved.

Library of Congress Cataloging-in-Publication Data

Habershon, Ada R. (Ada Ruth), 1861–1918.
  [Hidden Pictures]
  Types in the Old Testament / Ada R. Habershon

  Originally published: Hidden Pictures, or, How the New
Testament is Concealed in the Old Testament. London:
Oliphant, 1916.
  Includes index.

  1. Bible. N.T.—Relation to the Old Testament. 2. Typo-
logy (Theology) I. Title.
BS2387.H26   1988   221.6'4—dc19   88-12126

ISBN   0-8254-2856-4 (pbk.)

3 4 5 6 7 Printing/Year 92 91 90 89 88

Printed in the United States of America

CONTENTS

CONTENTS

INTRODUCTION

There are wonderful Bible stories, given to us by God Himself, that convey to us a hidden meaning. They are true stories. They not only tell us what happened long ago, this in itself would be quite interesting; many Old Testament scenes teach us something about the Lord Jesus Christ, the wonderful Saviour. Previews are given of His coming to earth and His death as a substitute for sinners. These hidden pictures are called *Types.*

The two most wonderful Bible Readings that were ever held took place on the same day—the first Easter Day, the first Lord's Day. They were conducted by the same Person, the risen Lord; one was held on a roadside on the way to Emmaus, the other in an Upper Room in Jerusalem. There were only two listeners at the first Bible Reading, but many others were present with them at the second. The subject was the same; on the Emmaus road, "Beginning at Moses and all the prophets, He expounded unto them in all the Scriptures the things concerning Himself" (Luke 24:27); and in the Upper Room He showed to them that "all things must be fulfilled, which were written in the law of Moses, and in the prophets, and in the Psalms, concerning Me. Then opened He their understanding, that they might understand the Scriptures" (vss. 44, 45).

The passages which He thus explained with such tender words and with such matchless power, so that their hearts burned within them as He was speaking, would not merely be the direct prophecies of Himself, not only the promises of His coming, but would include the hidden pictures and types which reveal so clearly why He must die. And though we have no full record of what He told them, we may, by the help of His Spirit, try to discover "the things concerning Himself," hidden away among the incidents and biographies of the Old Testament.

There are no stories like them. Even if they had been without a hidden meaning, they would have possessed irresistible attraction, but when we begin to discover why they were recorded for us by the inspiration of God's Spirit, and to see a little of their infinite meaning, we are fascinated by their beauty.

Through many years of study and Bible class teaching, I have always found that no subjects are of such unvarying interest to all sorts of audiences; high and low, rich and poor, young and old, boys in reformatories, girls in homes, women of varied social positions, all alike seem interested in the hidden pictures of the Old Testament. And this experience holds good in many places also, in America as well as in England, among women in the West End of London as well as in the East, while some of the Bible studies on the Types, having been translated into Italian and Spanish, have been used by missionaries and Christian workers in these countries.

It is a thrilling experience to tell these stories to some who have never before seen their meaning, and then, as you hint at the typical teaching and gradually unfold it, to see their faces lighting up with enjoyment and surprise, as much as to say, "I see it! Why did I never discover it before?" And if you are taking a very "difficult" class, speaking to those who need very gentle and tactful dealing, how delightful it is to lead up to the beautiful teaching about the Lord Jesus, and then bring in the practical lessons. To speak about abstract theology is impossible with such an audience, but by the help of these wonderful stories, the most ignorant may learn something "concerning Himself."

There is much danger in the present day of neglecting the Old Testament and confining both reading and study to the New Testament. The well-known lines of St. Augustine are too often forgotten:

"The New is in the Old concealed,
The Old is by the New revealed."

There are many passages in the New Testament that are not understood, because we are not sufficiently familiar with the Old Testament. "All Scripture is given by inspiration of God"—this includes the Old Testament—"and is profitable for doctrine, for reproof, for correction, for instruction in righteousness," and this includes the Old Testament.

The study of the Types is a certain antidote for error. It corrects our views on so many subjects. A young student in a theological college had a little book given to him on the Tabernacle and its teaching. He had never seen its meaning before, nor understood the reference in Hebrews to the "new and living Way through the Vail"; and when he caught a glimpse of the hidden beauties of Tabernacle teaching, his whole spiritual outlook was changed. He saw, as never before, his right of access; and the insidious attractions of so-called "higher criticism," and the doubts suggested by it were gone for ever.

The study of the Types is an unfailing antidote for this modern poison, for no one who has seen their beauty can doubt for a moment that the Scriptures are indeed, as they claim to be, the inspired Word of God.

The following Old Testament stories are but imperfectly told, and the hidden pictures but slightly outlined; it is my prayer that they may lead some needy souls to the feet of the Saviour. If they suggest to others the infinite beauty in these already familiar stories, and if Christian workers are induced to try this method of Bible class teaching, this little collection will not have been gathered together in vain, and He will be glorified.

"THINGS CONCERNING HIMSELF"

He made them understand the Book,
And from their eyes the veil He took,
The two disciples wond'ring look
    At "things concerning Himself."

He spoke of words they long had known,
But now they saw one Form alone,
The reason of His death was shown,
    By "things concerning Himself."

'Twas He inspired each sacred page,
For taught by Him from age to age,
One subject did each pen engage—
    "The things concerning Himself."

Oh may we too these secrets learn,
And when we to the Scriptures turn,
With opened hearts and minds discern,
    "The things concerning Himself."

ABEL'S LAMB

"By faith Abel offered unto God a more excellent sacrifice than Cain, by which he obtained witness that he was righteous, God testifying of his gifts; and by it he, being dead, yet speaketh."

Hebrews 11:4

1

ABEL'S LAMB

WHEN John the Baptist was talking to his two disciples, and saw the Lord Jesus coming towards him, he suddenly understood who He was, and said : " Behold the Lamb of God " (John i. 29, 36). What did he mean by giving Him such a strange title ? The Old Testament stories, such as the history of Cain and Abel, help us to understand what he meant.

These two brothers, Cain and Abel, both wanted to bring something to God, for they were what we should call very religious. They had been told by their parents, Adam and Eve, how they had been driven out of the beautiful Garden of Eden because of their disobedience, and how God had showed them that though they were sinners their sin could be put away. Cain and Abel knew that they were sinners too, but they had been told that if they brought something to God He would be pleased with them. They had been taught what He would like best, but Cain thought he would rather choose for himself, and so he worked hard in his garden and orchard, and brought a quantity of beautiful fruit.

Abel was a shepherd, and he went out to the flock and chose the most perfect lamb he could find. Then having killed it he laid it on an altar. Cain was much pleased with the pile of fruit on his altar. It really looked far more beautiful than the little dead lamb, for what could be more lovely than all sorts of ripe fruits with the bloom upon them !

I well remember a shop window which I saw in Chicago some years ago. A large shell-shaped basket was lying on its side as though it had just been upset, and the window was filled with peaches and pine-apples, pears and plums, grapes and melons. I am sure Cain's altar looked lovely, and he said to himself : " I've done my best."

But doing one's best is not enough for God. No one ever really does their best all the time, and if they could, it would not make them good enough to come into God's presence. Abel had learnt that he was a sinner and that he deserved to die, and that was why he brought the little lamb. He knew that doing his best was not good enough and that it would not get rid of a single sin. God had shown him this, and had told him that Another must die in his stead.

We know that God had taught him, for we read in the New Testament (Heb. xi. 4): "By *faith* Abel offered unto God a more excellent sacrifice than Cain." He could not have had faith unless he had heard, for "faith cometh by hearing"; and in the preceding chapter we have a hint of God's first teaching concerning the need of a sacrifice. "Unto Adam also and to his wife did the Lord God make coats of skins, and clothed them." In order to do this, that He might cover their nakedness on account of sin, an innocent animal had to die; and thus He taught them that they could only approach to Him through the shed blood.

The little lamb that died for Abel was a "type" of God's Son, Jesus Christ, who was to be sent by and by to die on the cross. "Without shedding of blood is no remission," that is, sin cannot be put away except by death. And so God showed to Cain and Abel that there was only one of the offerings with which He was pleased. Fire came down from heaven and burnt up the lamb on Abel's altar, but Cain's fruit was untouched.

Some people say that it was because Cain was wicked and Abel was good that God rejected Cain's fruit and accepted Abel's lamb; but those who say this have missed the type, and do not understand the meaning of the story.

There are a great many people even now like Cain. "For they being ignorant of God's righteousness, and going about to establish their own righteousness, have not submitted themselves unto the righteousness of God" (Rom. x. 3). They think that if they do their best they must be all right. The other day I heard a preacher say that he wondered who had invented the saying: "I'm doing my best"; and I thought to myself: "I know who it was, I am sure it was Cain."

Supposing God had said to us: "If you do your best every day, and all the day, all your life long, I will let you come to heaven when you die," do you think that any of us would get there? No, I am sure we should not. But that is not what He says. He tells us that we never have done our best, and cannot: "for all have sinned and come short of the glory of

God "; but that He has given His Best, His own Son, to die instead of us. Are you merely trying to do your best, or are you trusting in God's Best ?

We read in Jude that those who "have gone in the way of Cain" are like "clouds without water, carried about of winds." This seems a strange simile, but the writer was evidently thinking of a verse in the Book of Proverbs : "Whoso boasteth himself of a false gift is like clouds and wind without rain" (chap. xxv. 14). Cain boasted himself of a false gift, while Abel "obtained witness that he was righteous, God testifying of his gifts." Clouds without water may be good to look at, they may add to the beauty of the landscape, but they give no "showers of blessing," and aimlessly they drift along at the mercy of the winds.

When, long years afterwards, the children of Israel had been brought out of the land of bondage, and were about to enter into the land of promise, God gave them instructions about offering the very things that He rejected when brought by Cain. Why was this distinction made ? "When thou art come in unto the land which the Lord thy God giveth thee for an inheritance . . . thou shalt take of the first of all the fruit of the earth, which thou shalt bring of thy land that the Lord thy God giveth thee, and shalt put it in a basket, and shalt go unto the place which the Lord thy God shall choose to place His name there. . . . And the priest shall take the basket out of thine hand, and set it down *before the altar* of the Lord thy God" (Deut. xxvi. 1–4).   This was the secret.

It must be associated with the altar.   The blood had already been shed, the lamb had already been placed on the altar, and because of this God could look upon the first-fruits, and they could rejoice in every good thing which the Lord their God had given them (*v.* 11).

When our sins have been forgiven for His name's sake, then God will accept the fruit ; for the Lord Jesus said : " Herein is My Father glorified that ye bear much fruit, so shall ye be My disciples."

> " I will not work my soul to save,
>   For that my Lord has done ;
> But I will work like any slave,
>   For love of God's dear Son."

THE WEARY DOVE

"The dove found no rest for the sole of her foot, and she returned unto him into the ark; for the waters were on the face of the whole earth: then he put forth his hand, and took her, and pulled her in unto him into the ark."

Genesis 8:9

2

THE WEARY DOVE

MOST of us have known the history of Noah and the Ark since we were little children, but perhaps we never learnt then that his wonderful escape from the Flood was one of the stories with a hidden meaning, which are called "types."

Several hundreds of years had passed since Adam and Eve, Cain and Abel had died, and the world had become so wicked that God determined to punish men's sinfulness, and to drown them all with a terrible flood, so as to give the world a new beginning. Rain poured down in torrents from heaven, the seas and the rivers overflowed, and all were drowned except one family.

God had been very good to Noah, and had warned him beforehand and taught him the only way of escape. He told him how to make a big ship that would be able to float on the waters. So Noah set to work to build the Ark. How the people laughed at him through the long years that he was building it on dry land, probably far away from the sea. But he did not mind being laughed at, and went on with the work, all the time warning them about the flood that was coming, and urging them to come with him into the Ark ; for there would have been plenty of room for any who wanted to come.

We do not know whether Noah employed some of these men to help him, but if he did so, none of his carpenters took any notice of the warning. Knowing about the way of safety is not enough, for they were all drowned when at last the flood came. But before one drop of rain fell, God said to Noah : " Come into the Ark " ; and he and his wife, and his sons and daughters-in-law obeyed, and were perfectly safe ; for " the Lord shut him in."

The Ark is a beautiful picture of the Lord Jesus Christ, who came to save us from a worse judgment than the flood. God says " Come " and take refuge in Him ; and if we do so we are quite, quite safe. " The wrath to come " will never touch one of us who have obeyed the words of the Saviour : " Come unto Me."

The Ark met the waters breaking on it, but Noah and his family were just as safe as the Ark itself. The Lord Jesus bore all the waves of God's wrath against sin, but we who trust in Him are as safe as He is. Sometimes we get laughed at if we talk to people about the Lord Jesus, but the laughter will not hurt us. Supposing that Noah had stopped building the Ark because people laughed at him, he would have been drowned as well as they.

There is another beautiful lesson in this story. Noah himself becomes a picture of the Lord Jesus. When the rain had ceased, and the flood was going down, he opened the window and let fly two birds. The first was a raven, and it flew over the waters and soon saw some of the dead bodies floating about. A raven can feed on such things, and so it did not want to come back. But next Noah sent out a dove. How gladly she flew away! It was so delightful to be free after having been shut up for nearly six months in the Ark. The air seemed so fresh, and the sun was beginning to break out from the clouds as away she flew. Free at last, no one to tell her which way to go, she might fly north, south, east, or west, just as she pleased. It was indeed delightful. But presently she began to get just a little bit tired, and she looked about for land, but she could only see water—water on every side. There were some dead bodies.floating about, but she turned away from these.

That which satisfied the raven would not satisfy her. "The dove found no rest for the sole of her foot." On and on she flew, and at last her wings began to droop. She thought: "I can't go on like this much longer. I had better go back to Noah and to the Ark." And so "she returned unto him into the Ark." But she did not fly so quickly now. Oh, how tired she was! At last she saw the Ark, a mere speck in the distance, and she was glad, so glad to see it again. But it was a long, long way off, and she began to think she would never reach it.

Noah was at his window watching her as she flew wearily back, and just as she reached the Ark, and it seemed as though she would drop into the water, he leaned out of the window, " put forth his hand and took her, and pulled her in unto him," or " caused her to come in unto him into the Ark."

Have you ever felt like that tired dove? Many a boy or girl thinks how splendid it will be to be free when they leave school ; or perhaps they leave home and come up to London, and they say to themselves: "Now at last I can do just what I like." At first it does seem delightful to go their own way, but soon, like the dove, they begin to get tired. It is a happy thing for them if they do just as the dove did and fly to the Ark. The Lord Jesus is looking out for those who are weary and who cannot find a resting-place ; and He is just waiting to put out His hand so as to cause them to come in unto Him. He says: "Come unto Me, all ye that labour and are heavy laden, and I will give you rest." But He is not far away, as the Ark was when the little dove began to feel so tired. "The Lord is at hand," so near that He can hear the faintest whisper, the softest sigh. And everyone who comes to Him is so glad to confess : "The Lord was ready to save me."

David sighed : "Oh that I had wings like a dove ! for then would I fly away and be at rest. Lo, then would I wander far off and remain in the wilderness." But if he had gained his desire he would have found it just as unsatisfying as Noah's dove found it.

We long to the wilderness place to fly,
And : "Oh for the wings of a dove" we cry,

We think if we only could hide away,
And far from the rush and the turmoil stray,
That then we could quietly rest awhile,
Apart from the world from its frown or smile.
The wilderness is not the place of rest,
Nor will it be thus that our hearts are blest !
No rest for the sole of our feet we find,
But like that lone dove with the Ark behind
We wander about with a wearied wing,
Unable to find any earthly thing
On which we can rest ; till we turn at length
And fly to the Ark with our failing strength.
Ah, now we have found an abiding rest !
The outstretchèd Hand is our shelter blest,
And leaving behind us the desert waste,
With ioy of that sheltering love we taste.

THE FATHER
AND THE SON

"Isaac spoke unto Abraham his father, and said, My father: and he said, Here am I, my son. And he said, Behold the fire and the wood: but where is the lamb for a burnt offering? And Abraham said, My son, God will provide Himself a lamb for a burnt offering: so they went both of them together."

Genesis 22:7,8

3

THE FATHER AND THE SON

ABRAHAM had one son, Isaac, who was very precious to him. He was the heir to all God's promises, for when God had brought Abraham into the land of Canaan He promised to give it to Abraham and his descendants, though at that time he had no son. It was not until he was an old man that Isaac was born. Great was the rejoicing over the child of promise, and as he grew up he became more and more precious to his father.

There was only one in all the tents of Abraham that did not love the little child, and this was Ishmael, a boy fourteen years older than Isaac. Though Abraham was his father, he was not the true seed about whom the promises were given, for he was the son of an Egyptian slave-woman. He behaved so badly to Isaac that at last Abraham was obliged to

send him and his mother away. As we read
the account in the Book of Genesis we should
never think that this part of the story of Isaac
was a type, but the meaning was revealed to
the Apostle Paul.

The two children represented the difference
between living under the law and being born
again under grace. Those who believe on the
Lord Jesus become God's own children. They
are born from above, into His own family, and
nothing they do can alters the fact. God will
not turn them out because of bad behaviour, as
Abraham turned out Ishmael, for they do not
become His children because they have kept
the law : " But as many as received Him (the
Lord Jesus), to them gave He power to become
the sons of God, even to them that believe
on His name."   So Paul adds : " Now we,
brethren, as Isaac was, are the children of
promise " (Gal. iv. 28).

There is one event in the story of Isaac
which contains a very beautiful hidden picture,
and here we see in Abraham a type of God
the Father.

Abraham had such strong faith that when
God gave a promise he trusted Him implicitly,
but his faith was very sorely tried. God Him-

self tested it, for He told Abraham to take his only son Isaac, whom he so dearly loved, and offer him up for a burnt offering.   How startled Abraham must have been at such a command, but he did not hesitate.   We know from the New Testament that he made up his mind to obey the command, feeling sure that God would still fulfil His promise of giving the land to Isaac's descendants.   Unbelief might have whispered : " If you kill Isaac, it will be impossible for that promise to be fulfilled," but faith obeyed, " accounting that God was able to raise him up " (Heb. xi. 19).

God had told Abraham that the offering was to be made at one certain spot among the mountains of Moriah, far away from the tents of Abraham.   God was always very particular about His types, and in order to make them as perfect as possible, events which were hidden pictures had to take place in special localities, so as to link them with other events and other hidden pictures (see p. 195).

Strong faith obeys promptly, so early the next morning Abraham set out on his journey with Isaac, having first cut the wood that would be needed for the burnt offering.   On the third day they saw the hills of Moriah in the distance, and God told Abraham that this was the place. All through Old Testament days God Himself "saw the place afar off" where His own Son would be offered up.

Abraham left the two young men at the foot of the hill, and told them to stay there with the ass. He said that he and his son were going to worship God, and so sure was he that God would give Isaac back again to him, that he added : "I and the lad will . . . come again to you."

The scene is full of typical teaching, for it is a picture of how the Father "spared not His own Son, but delivered Him up for us all." Because this was a type, Abraham had to journey to the very land, "the land of Moriah," where long years afterwards the Lord was crucified on one of the same hills. On one part of Mount Moriah the Temple of Jerusalem was built, and the altar set up where the offering of God's only begotten Son was so constantly typified ; and Calvary itself must have formed part of the same range of hills.

Isaac willingly accompanied his father. Twice we read the words : "They went both of them together." There was perfect harmony and trust between them, though Isaac evidently did not understand what was to happen. How much greater was the perfect unity between God the Father and God the Son. They always "went both of Them together." There is a certain kind of teaching which seems to imply that God is an angry God, who has to be reconciled to man at the urgent entreaty of His Son, but we must never forget that it was God Himself who devised the plan whereby He could save the sinner. "God so loved the world that He gave His only begotten Son." "They went both of Them together."

And so we see Abraham and Isaac setting out. Abraham takes the fire and the knife in his own hand, while the wood is laid upon Isaac, reminding us that the Lord Jesus went down into the valley and climbed the hill "bearing His cross" (John xix. 17). It was not the first time that Abraham had offered a sacrifice to God. Isaac probably had seen him do it frequently, but in the preparation on this occasion he noticed one omission, and he said to his father : " My father. . . . Behold the fire and the wood : but where is the lamb for a burnt offering ? " This question seems to echo throughout all the Old Testament days.

"Where is the Lamb ? " There were

many lambs, but they only prefigured THE
LAMB.   When we come to the New Testa-
ment the question is answered, as John the
Baptist points to the Lord Jesus and says :
" Behold the Lamb of God."   And it is to
Him that Abraham's answer points.   " My son,
God will provide Himself a lamb for a burnt
offering."   This must have been one of the
times of which the Lord Jesus spoke when He
said : " Your father Abraham rejoiced to see My
day, and he saw it and was glad " (John viii. 56).
" God shall provide *Himself*."   God *Himself*
must provide the offering ; and He provides
Him not only to meet our need but *for Himself*,
that He may satisfy His own righteous claims ;
nay, more, we know that *He Himself* became
the Lamb, that He might die for us.

When they came to the place, Abraham
bound his son, who, without a murmur, submitted to being laid upon the altar.   Abraham
must have loved him all the more for his ready
acquiescence.   " Therefore doth My Father
love Me, because I lay down My life " (John
x. 17).   But here the type fails or changes, for
a substitute is found for Isaac, as a Substitute
has been found for us who believe on the Lord
Jesus.   The Angel of the Lord tells Abraham

to stay his hand. The testing is sufficient. Abraham has shown that he will obey God at any cost ; and as he lifts up his eyes he sees a ram caught in the thicket. Here is the lamb provided by God as Isaac's substitute—but none was found for the Lord Jesus !

Abraham calls the name of the place " Jehovah-jireh," which means, " The Lord will see" or " provide." For Him to see the need means that He will provide that which will meet it, and these words follow : " In the Mount of the Lord it shall be seen." At the cross we see how God Himself has provided the Lamb. The words " Jehovah-jireh" are often used out of their connection, but it must not be forgotten that they refer in the first instance to the One whom God has provided. We often hear the words applied to the daily provision which He makes for us. We sing :—

> "Yet one thing secures us whatever betide,
> The Scripture assures us the Lord will provide."

And this is indeed true, but do we not often forget the best part of it, that the title was given in connection with the Lamb ? " My son, God will provide Himself a lamb." The less is included in the greater, as in Romans

viii. 32 : " He that spared not His own Son, but delivered Him up for us all, how shall He not *WITH HIM* also freely give us all things ? "

" Jehovah-jireh " is rightly applied to the " all things," but we must not forget the best gift of all—God's unspeakable Gift—which includes all the rest.   The necessaries of life and all the other blessings are only provided " with Him."

A BRIDE
FOR ISAAC

"They called Rebekah, and said unto her, Wilt thou go with this man? And she said, I will go."

Genesis 24:58

4

A BRIDE FOR ISAAC

THE tents of Abraham were pitched among heathen nations who worshipped other gods, and when the time came to seek a bride for Isaac, Abraham determined to send into Mesopotamia, to the relatives he had left behind when he forsook his country at the call of God. He could not allow his son to take a wife from among the idolatrous Canaanites, so he summoned his most trusted servant, generally supposed to have been the Eliezer mentioned in Gen. xv. 2, and sent him forth with full instructions. " Supposing she does not want to follow me into this land," asked the servant, " what am I to do ? Must I come back to fetch Isaac to join her in the land from which you came out ?" " Ah no," said Abraham, " Isaac must never go back. ' Beware thou that thou bring not my son thither again ' " (Gen. xxiv. 6, 8).

And so the little caravan started on the long journey. There were ten camels with their drivers, and most of the camels were laden with rich presents for the future bride. We do not read anything of what happened on the way, but Abraham's servant had learnt the secret that makes a man a really prosperous traveller. He could say: "I being in the way, the Lord led me" (v. 27). He knew it was right for him to set forth ; he was " in the way " that God meant him to go, and so he had committed the whole journey, and every detail connected with it, into God's hand. Any one who can do this is sure to be a good traveller.

When at last he came to the city of Nahor, Abraham's brother, and halted his camels at the well just outside the city, he felt a special need for fresh guidance. It was evening, the hour when the women in the East were accustomed to come out to draw water from their well. Would Isaac's bride be amongst them ? How was Abraham's servant to know her ? He did not want to make a mistake, so he asked God to give him a sign that he might be quite sure about it.

Asking for a sign is generally a token of unbelief, but in this case it was the opposite, for it showed how strong his faith was, and how thoroughly he depended on God. And the sign was given. He requested that the maiden from whom he asked water, if she were the appointed bride, might at once answer: "Drink, and I will give thy camels drink also." As he prayed he looked at the faces of the damsels that came to the well ; and soon his eye lighted upon one who was very beautiful. Perhaps he detected a likeness to Abraham, but instantly he felt assured that this was she.

He watched her descend the steps of the well and draw water, and as she came up again he ran forward eagerly, and asked for a drink of water. Immediately she said : " Drink, my lord," and lowered her pitcher from her head or her shoulder, and gave him to drink ; and when he was refreshed she added the other words that he had asked for in his prayer, and said : "I will draw water for thy camels also, until they have done drinking." Abraham's servant watched her filling her pitcher again and again and emptying it into the trough ; and he wondered, as we always do when we get a striking answer to prayer.

He said nothing at present about his errand, but he gave her a beautiful ornament of gold for her forehead, and two heavy gold bracelets, for he thought: "Surely this is she." And when he asked her who she was, and found that she was actually the granddaughter of Nahor, he bowed his head and worshipped God, for his heart was glad to think how he had evidently been led to the very one appointed for Isaac.

But this is not only a very beautiful story; it is also a wonderful hidden picture of the work of the Holy Spirit, who has been sent forth by God the Father to call out a "people for His name," for the One who has already passed through death and resurrection, as Isaac had done "in a figure" (see Heb. xi. 19 and p. 21). The One sent is the Father's eldest Servant, who is always ready to do His work. His directions are very clear. The bride of Isaac is to be brought right out of the land in which she dwells. Isaac's place is not there. As Mr. Spurgeon once said: "The Lord Jesus Christ headed the grand emigration party which has come right out of the world."

We are told that the servant did not go empty-handed, but took with him samples of the riches of Abraham and Isaac: "All the goods of his master were in his hand." When the Holy Spirit came down, He, too, brought

with Him an earnest of the inheritance which
they who listen to His message would receive, for
He Himself is the earnest.   Abraham's servant
asks Rebekah if there is room for him in her
father's house, and she at once replies that there
is plenty of room for them all.   Had she
refused, he would never have been able to tell
her about Isaac.

When he is admitted, his first thought is of
his errand : " I will not eat until I have told
mine errand " (v. 33).   He never forgets it, and
his object, like that of Him whom he fore-
shadows, is to speak of him who sent him,
of the father and of the son.   " When the
Comforter is come, whom I will send unto
you from the Father, even the Spirit of truth,
which proceedeth from the Father, He shall
testify of Me."   " He shall not speak of
Himself" (John xv. 26 ; xvi. 13).

So Abraham's servant tells about his master,
his master's son, and all his possessions, and
gives to Rebekah some of the precious things
which he has brought.   " The Lord hath
blessed my master greatly, and he is become
great " : and unto his son " hath he given all
that he hath."   In the Gospel of John we read
again : " The Father loveth the Son, and hath

given all things into His hand" : and again :
"All things that the Father hath are Mine."

But there was one more thing that Isaac
needed. He could not enjoy these things alone :
as God had said of Adam : "It is not good that
the man should be alone ; I will make him an
helpmeet for him." The business of the servant
was to fetch Rebekah. He therefore took that
which was Isaac's and showed it to Rebekah, to
prove the truth of his words about Isaac's
riches. "He shall receive of Mine, and shall
show it unto you." He also promised blessing
to her in Isaac, and he showed her "things to
come."

Her friends, while consenting to her union
with Isaac, would have detained her, but there
must be no delay. "Hinder me not," he says
to them, when they suggest her waiting at least
ten days. "The Holy Ghost saith, To-day"
(Heb. iii. 7), and this is ever His cry : "Behold
now is the accepted time." And so the question is put to Rebekah. She must make the
great decision. Does she believe what she has
heard ? Is she satisfied that Isaac really wants
her to go to him ? Is she willing to trust herself to the guidance of the one who has come to
fetch her ? "Wilt thou go with this man ? "

she is asked, and she promptly replies : " I will go."

She believes the report he has brought her, and " forgetting those things which are behind, and reaching forth unto those things which are before, (she presses) toward the mark for the prize of the high calling " (Phil. iii. 13, 14)— which is, that she shall be the bride of Isaac.

She leaves the old home, and forgetting her own people and her father's house (Ps. xlv. 10), sets out on the desert journey under the guidance of the one who has come to fetch her. We read in Gen. xxiv. 61 that she " followed the man ; and the servant took Rebekah, and went his way."   It was the right way, we may be sure, for he knew just the best road to take, having travelled that way before ; and it was not likely that Rebekah tried to choose her own path—she was satisfied to be guided.   Thus we also may be led by the Spirit of God.

We can imagine that during the journey, and at the various stopping-places, she would delight in questioning him about Isaac, and would want to learn more about the one to whom she was going.   We are not told anything about those conversations, only one question and answer are given ; but they are characteristic of the whole. As she nears the end of the journey and sees Isaac in the distance she asks : " What man is this ? " " My master," is the answer. From first to last this is the servant's one theme. He does not speak of himself, but only speaks of Isaac, till at last he is able to bring her right into his presence.

The type is so plain that none can fail to see its beauty. We too have to make the decision as to whether we will go with this Servant, and when, having believed the message, we say with Rebekah, " I will go," we too are led by the faithful Guide through the desert journey, till by and by we see Him face to face.

> " Oh the blessed joy of meeting—
>   All the desert past !
> Oh the wondrous words of greeting
>   He shall speak at last ! "

Isaac meanwhile was waiting for his bride ; and we are told two things about him : the one, that he came to meet her from the well Lahai-roi, where he dwelt (Gen. xxiv. 62 ; xxv. 11), " the well of Him that liveth and seeth me " (Gen. xvi. 14) ; the other, that as she was journeying he " went out to meditate in the field at the eventide," or (margin) " to pray."

The words of Isaac's prayer are not given ;
but we have the record of another prayer, offered
by One who ever dwelt in the presence of God,
and who pleads for those who are journeying to
Him through the wilderness, and this is what
He said : " Holy Father, keep through Thine
own Name those whom Thou hast given Me " ;
" The glory which Thou gavest Me I have
given them " ; " Father, I will that they also,
whom Thou hast given Me, be with Me where
I am, that they may behold My glory " (John
xvii. 11, 22, 24).

The chapter ends with the assurance of
Isaac's satisfaction and love : " He loved her."
The story falls far short of the Antitype, for
Isaac did not have to bear anything in order to
win her for his bride ; but He whom he fore-
shadows " shall see of the travail of His soul
and shall be satisfied."

John xvii. illustrated by the Brides of Scripture

Eve, the bride of *Adam*, was given to him (Gen. ii. 22 ;
John xvii. 6). She was one with him (Gen. ii. 23 ;
John xvii. 21, 23).

Rebekah, the bride of *Isaac*, was fetched from her
home and kindred (Gen. xxiv. 4–8). " Out of

the world " (John xvii. 6, 16). She was taught
that Abraham had given to Isaac "all that he
hath " (Gen. xxiv. 36). "Now they have known
that all things whatsoever Thou hast given Me
are of Thee " (John xvii. 7). Isaac prayed as
she journeyed (Gen. xxiv. 63). " I pray for them
. . . that Thou shouldest keep them " (John
xvii. 9, 15).

Rachel, the bride of *Jacob*, was won by his long service
(Gen. xxix. 20).

Ruth, the bride of *Boaz*, was his by redemption and a
finished work (Ruth iii. 18 ; iv. 14).

Michal, the bride of *David*, was the reward of his
victory (1 Sam. xvii. 25). " I have finished the
work which Thou gavest Me to do " (John
xvii. 4).

Zipporah, the bride of *Moses*, became his after he had
laid aside his princely glory (Ex. ii. 21). " The
glory which I had with Thee before the world
was " (John xvii. 5).

The *Shulamite* was the object of *Solomon's* love and
desire (Song of Solomon vii. 10 ; ii. 16 ; John
xvii. 10, 24).

Esther, the bride of *Ahasuerus*, saw the glory of the
king (Esther v. 1). " That they may behold My
glory " (John xvii. 24).

STORY OF
THE SEVEN DREAMS

"Can we find such a one as this is, a man in whom the Spirit of God is? ... Go unto Joseph; what he saith to you, do."

Genesis 41:38, 55b

5

STORY OF THE SEVEN DREAMS

THE beautiful story of Joseph is not only very interesting in itself, but is one of the most striking of the types, for it is a wonderful picture of the life and work of the Lord Jesus Christ. Joseph was one of a large family, for he had eleven brothers, and as he was a special favourite with his father Jacob the others were very jealous. To make matters worse, he one night had two dreams, in which he saw himself a great ruler and his father and brothers bowing down before him. He knew in his heart that God had sent these dreams to show him what was to happen, but when he told them to his brothers they were very angry, and determined to prevent them from coming true.

One day their opportunity came, as they thought, for Joseph was sent by his father with a message to them as they were feeding their flocks a long way from home. They saw him coming over the hills and exclaimed: " Here comes the dreamer, now we'll see if his dreams will come true ! " Some of his brethren would have liked to kill him, but the others, who were not so cruel, suggested that he should be lowered into a pit. To this they agreed, and after they had cast him into the pit they sat down to take their meal. It had probably been delayed by the long discussion. While they were sitting thus some camels appeared in the distance, and as they drew nearer Joseph's brothers could tell that it was a caravan of merchants going down to Egypt to sell their spices.

" Now," they said, " we can get rid of this brother of ours. We will sell him to these Ishmaelites." And soon they were bargaining with them as to the price, till at last Joseph was sold as a slave for twenty pieces of silver and carried far away from his father's house. His brothers thought that this was an end of the dreams, but it was really part of God's way of making them come true. When the merchants arrived in Egypt, they quickly sold Joseph to an officer in the army of Pharaoh, King of Egypt, and he became his servant.

Joseph was only seventeen years old when all this happened, and during the thirteen years he was a slave he must often have thought of his father, of his favourite brother Benjamin, and of the old home.   But before his troubles came he had learned to trust God ; and though he was a slave, people soon began to find out that God was with him.   He was so faithful in all he did that his master proved that he could be trusted, and things went well when Joseph was looking after them.

Even thus far in the story we can see a great many things which remind us of the Lord Jesus.   He too was the Well-beloved of His Father :   His brethren, the sons of Israel or Jacob, hated Him " without a cause " ; they envied Him, and at last tried to get rid of Him by nailing Him to the cross.   He had left His Father's house when He " took upon Him the form of a servant " ; but God was with Him all the time.   He too was sold for the price of a slave, thirty pieces of silver.   God had promised that the Lord Jesus should sit on a throne and reign over this world, and this promise has never yet been fulfilled ; but it will be one day, as surely as Joseph's dreams were fulfilled.

When Joseph had been cast into the pit and

sold as a slave, it did not seem at all likely that those dreams would come true, and so we read in one of the Psalms : " Until the time that his word came to pass, the word of the Lord tried him " (Ps. cv. 19, R.V.).

But Joseph had to go one step lower. He was put in prison because he refused to sin against God, and a false accusation was brought against him. He must often have wondered through all those thirteen years how the dreams were to come true.

But the Lord Jesus went down even lower than this, for He went into the pit of death and the prison-house of the grave. We read in the same Psalm that in the prison they hurt Joseph's feet with fetters, but they pierced the feet of the Lord Jesus with the cruel nails, and that was far worse.

Joseph had two fellow-prisoners, and this reminds us that when the Lord Jesus was crucified there were with Him two others who were evil-doers, or malefactors. There had evidently been some plot in the palace of Pharaoh—perhaps an attempt on his life—and the head cook and the chief butler were imprisoned. One night they each had a dream ; and when Joseph, who had been made one of

the warders of the prison, came in to them
in the morning he found them looking very
troubled.

They did not know what the dreams signi-
fied, but Joseph was able to tell them. He
showed them that the chief cook's dream meant
that in three days he would be put to death,
and that the chief butler's dream meant that
Pharaoh was going to restore him to his post
in the palace, and he was once more to wait on
the king. So Joseph had a message of death
for one and a message of life for the other, just
as the Lord on the cross had a beautiful promise
for one of the robbers : " To-day shalt thou be
with Me in Paradise." In three days their
dreams came true, but still Joseph's own dreams
were unfulfilled. As his fellow-prisoners went
forth, the one to judgment and to death, and
the other to life in the king's court, Joseph's
faith must have been very much tried ; and yet
he must have thought to himself : " Their
dreams have come true, and so will mine."

The way to the throne was through the
prison-house, and he had only to wait God's time.
The Lord Jesus had to go to the cross first, but
by and by He will sit upon His throne. As
He said to His two disciples on the road to

Emmaus, on the day He rose from the dead, when they were so perplexed because the promises had not come true : " Ought not Christ to have suffered these things, and to enter into His glory ? " Who would have thought that all that Joseph suffered was God's way of bringing to pass the thing He had planned ?

It was through his fellow-prisoner that he was at last brought before the notice of the king. Joseph had begged the butler to remember him when he was set free, and to say a word to the king for him ; but when he got back to the palace he tried to forget all about the days he had spent in prison, and he thought no more about Joseph. " Yet did not the chief butler remember Joseph, but forgat him."

But soon something happened which made him remember. Pharaoh had two dreams, and neither he nor anyone else in the palace could tell what they meant. " I had a dream once," said the butler ; " I am ashamed to say it was when I was in prison, but there was a young man there, a Hebrew, who told me exactly what it meant, and it all came true as he had said." This was enough for Pharaoh.

He sent to fetch Joseph out of the prison, and he was very quickly brought before him.

And now the fulfilment of Joseph's dreams is coming very near.   The two dreams of his fellow-prisoners and the two dreams of Pharaoh were links in the chain leading to this wonderful result.

When Pharaoh told Joseph his dreams, Joseph at once saw that God had sent them to prepare him for what was coming.   The land of Egypt depends on the river Nile for its harvests.   If there is plenty of rain the river overflows and waters the land, making the soil of the fields rich with the mud it leaves behind. Pharaoh dreamt that seven fat cattle came up out of the river, and God showed Joseph that this meant that there would be seven years of wonderful harvests.   But the seven lean cattle that came up after them meant that they would be followed by seven years of famine.   The dream of the seven good and the seven bad ears of corn told the same story.

Joseph not only interpreted the dreams but advised Pharaoh what to do to prepare for the famine ; and Pharaoh was so pleased with him and his wisdom that he made him ruler over the whole land, to carry out the plans which he had suggested.   Everyone in Egypt was told to bow down before Joseph.   The heralds ran before his chariot crying : " Bow the knee."

During the seven years of plenty we may be sure that Joseph was very busy giving orders for storing up the large quantities of corn, and when the famine came there was plenty in his storehouses.   Very soon the people in Egypt began to feel the pinch of hunger, and they appealed to the king.   But he sent them to the only one who could supply their need. " Go to Joseph," was his reply to everyone ; " and Joseph opened all the storehouses," and sold the corn to all who came.   No one was refused.

So here again we see in Joseph a type of the Lord Jesus, who has been exalted by God and " given a Name which is above every name, that at the Name of Jesus every knee should bow."   This will really be fulfilled by and by ; but to-day He is the One who can feed souls, and satisfy all hungry hearts.   When we come to God and tell Him that we long for peace and for the pardon of our sins, He tells us to go to the Lord Jesus, for He is the only One through whom we can get what we need.   When we do go to Him He opens all His storehouses as

Joseph did, and gives us as much as we can carry (Gen. xliv. 1).

But though the people of Egypt bowed down before Joseph, his father and brothers had not done so as yet, and so his dream had not yet come true, though it was more than twenty years since he had been sold as a slave. The famine was very bad in other countries, and soon the news spread that there was corn in Egypt, so that from all parts the people thronged the palace and the storehouses of Joseph. He must have looked out every day for his brothers, and at last he saw them amongst the crowds. He knew them at once, but they did not know him, till the second time they came he made himself known to them. How frightened they were when they found that the brother they had treated so cruelly twenty years ago was ruler over all the land of Egypt!

When the Lord Jesus was living here on earth, His own people, the descendants of these very men, did not know Him. " He came unto His own, and His own received Him not." They did not believe on Him, but treated Him more cruelly than even Joseph's brothers had treated him, for they put Him to death. And still the Jews, as we call the children of Israel now, have not as a nation believed on the Lord Jesus, though all these years hungry souls from other nations have been coming to His storehouses.

Joseph was delighted to see his brothers at last, and he gladly invited them to come and live near him ; but first he sent them home to fetch Jacob their father and all their families. When Jacob heard their story he was afraid to start on the journey. He could not believe that Joseph, the son he had lost so long ago, was really alive ; but when he saw the wagons full of the good things he had sent he began to believe it. God also sent him a dream to set his heart at rest, so that he was no longer afraid to go to his son ; and this, the seventh dream in the story, is the last link in the chain. Everything was changed when he learned that Joseph was really alive and was looking out for him to come and live with him. Everything is changed for us too when we learn that the Lord Jesus, who died on the cross such a long time ago, is really alive in heaven, that He is looking out for us to come to Him for food, and that He wants us to live with Him for ever.

The whole family settled in the land of Goshen, the very best part of Egypt. But

Joseph had one more thing to make him sad.
When his father died his brothers sent him such
a strange message ! They had never really believed that he had forgiven them, and thought
that now at last he would punish them for
having been so unkind ; and so they pretended
that Jacob had left a message asking him to
forgive them.   He was much grieved at this.

He might have said to them, as the Lord
Jesus said to one of His disciples : " Have I been
so long time with you, and yet hast thou not
known Me ? " Joseph told his brothers that
they were not to be sorry any more.   Though
they had meant to do him harm, God had sent
him down into Egypt to be their deliverer,
and not only theirs but the deliverer of the
Egyptians and of others as well.   When the
children of Israel see the Lord Jesus and mourn
at the way they have treated Him, He too will
show how He freely forgives them ; and He
will make them understand that though they
put Him to death it was God's way of making
Him the Saviour for the whole world.

The corn that Joseph had stored up lasted
all through the famine, but when the people
had no more money they came to him in great
distress.   " What are we to do ? " they said.

" Our money is gone, there is nothing left but our bodies.   Will you buy us, and go on feeding us ? "

" Nothing but our bodies."   That is all we have to offer to the Lord Jesus, but it is just what He wants.   We have no money that we could offer Him, and He does not want any, for what He gives is "without money and without price."   But He wants *US*.   Joseph bought the people, and gave them not only food for themselves, but said to them : "Lo ! here is seed for you, and ye shall sow the land."

When we have been saved by the Lord Jesus He wants us to "present our bodies" to Him (Rom. xii. 1).   They belong rightly to Him, for He has bought us, but He wants to have us as His willing servants ; and when He has given us food for our hearts, by teaching us something about His love, He tells us to go and scatter the seed which He provides—" seed to the sower, and bread to the eater."

"BRING THESE MEN HOME"

‘‘Joseph said to the ruler of his house, Bring these men home.’’

Genesis 43:16a

6

"BRING THESE MEN HOME"

THERE is one incident in the history of Joseph and his brethren which gives us a beautiful picture of the work of the Holy Spirit, both now and in days to come. Joseph's brethren had come down into Egypt a second time, bringing Benjamin with them, as Joseph had commanded ; but they had not yet recognised Joseph. When Joseph saw the brother he so much loved, his heart was full, and he said to the ruler of his house : "Bring these men home." The feast was to be prepared at once,—" Slay and make ready " was the order,— for his brethren were to sit down and eat with him.

The chief of all his servants did as Joseph bade him, and brought the men to Joseph's house ; but their hearts were filled with fear. They did not know him yet, and thought of him only as a stern and imperious judge ; so

they were very thankful to pour out their troubles
into the ears of one who had such authority :
" They communed with him at the door of the
house," before they came to the banqueting-
house. They told how their money, the price
of the corn they had bought on their first visit,
had been returned to them, and how they were
troubled at heart at finding it.

The steward comforts them, and says : "Peace
be to you, fear not." Then he provides them
with water that they may wash their feet, and
with provender for their asses, and when they
have been made ready he brings them into
Joseph's presence, and they feast with him.
But in the next chapter we find the steward is
once more sent forth by Joseph. First of all,
he is told to " fill the men's sacks with food, as
much as they can carry," and again the money
is to be returned in the sack's mouth, and the
cup of Joseph is to be placed in the sack of
Benjamin.

Joseph cannot reveal himself to his brethren
till they have been convicted of sin ; and so,
when they are not far from the city, Joseph
sends his steward after them : " Up, follow
after the men." When he overtook them
he was to accuse them of stealing Joseph's

cup, search was to be made for it, and the one
with whom it was found was to be brought
back to be Joseph's slave.   The brothers were
quite sure that none of them had the cup, and
great was their dismay when it was found in
Benjamin's sack.   They could not return home
without him, for they had promised their father
Jacob that they would take the greatest care of
his youngest son, and Judah had become surety
for his safety; and so they turn their faces to
Joseph's palace and return again to the city,
trembling with fear at the thought of appearing
before him.

So many misfortunes seem to have happened to them that they wonder if it is
because of that sin long ago, their cruel treatment of their brother Joseph, their lies to their
father Jacob.   It has all come so vividly before
them in this their time of distress, and as they
fall before Joseph they are ready to own
their sin, little thinking that he before whom
they have been brought is the very one whom
they tried so hard to get rid of.   When they
first heard his dreams they thought only of the
humiliation of bowing down to him.   They
were to realise now that it meant salvation to
them, for he it was that had delivered them

from starvation.   And so they fall before him in deep distress, little knowing how his heart is yearning over them.

Judah is spokesman for the rest.   " How shall we clear ourselves ? " he says ;   " God hath found out the iniquity of thy servants " ;   and then he pleads for Benjamin and for their sorrowing father in the homeland.   Joseph cannot refrain himself any longer, and we have seen how he made himself known.   But in this portion of the story we may see a foreshadowing of the Holy Spirit's work in bringing sinners to the Lord Jesus.

He has been commanded to bring certain men "home."   He speaks to the heart.   He comforts.   He says : " Peace be to you."   He says : " Fear not."   It is He who in the Word provides the water in which we can wash our feet, before we enter the presence of the Lord, to feast with Him.   It is He who gives us sackfuls of corn, as much as we can carry. But first, His work is to convict of sin, for the One whom Joseph typifies can only reveal Himself to them who thus come to Him.

The forgotten sins of long ago come to the memory and become a heavy burden.   But just as Joseph comforted his brethren and besought

them to believe in his forgiveness, so the Lord
Jesus speaks peace and pardon to the troubled
heart that owns its sin. But first there must be
the Servant's work, the Spirit's work, which
leads to a remembrance of sin.

We also see in this a hidden picture of the
future work of the Holy Spirit amongst the
descendants of Jacob, the children of Israel.
They did not recognise their Messiah when He
came to this earth, but, as Stephen tells us, "at
the second time Joseph was made known to his
brethren"; and "the second time," when He
comes again to this earth, Israel will know their
Messiah. But before this they will have to be
convicted of their sin, and the great Servant will
once more do His work.

"I will pour upon the house of David, and
upon the inhabitants of Jerusalem, the spirit of
grace and of supplications; and they shall look
upon Me whom they have pierced (as Joseph's
brethren looked upon the one whom they had
sold into Egypt), and they shall mourn for
Him" (Zech. xii. 10); mourn that long ago
they had tried to get rid of Him. Then He
will comfort them as Joseph comforted his
brethren, and will show them that their sin
is all forgiven, and they will exclaim at last:

"He was wounded for our transgressions, He was bruised for our iniquities ; the chastisement of our peace was upon Him, and with His stripes we are healed" (Isa. liii. 5).

In the parable of the great supper (Luke xiv. 16–24) we have similar teaching about the Holy Spirit. The servant is sent forth to summon the guests. He is told to " bring them in "—to " compel them to come in." The maimed, the halt, and the blind are those who cannot come alone, for they need to be carried or led. None but the Holy Spirit can " bring " such, can " compel them to come," and none but He can say to His Master : "Lord, it is done as Thou hast commanded, and yet there is room."

These things are not said of the servants who invite the guests to the marriage feast in Matthew xxii., for this describes the work of God's people instead of the work of the one Servant.

THE PASSOVER

"When I see the blood, I will pass over you."

Exodus 12:13b

"For even Christ our Passover is sacrificed for us."

1 Corinthians 5:7b

7

THE PASSOVER

"EVEN Christ our Passover is sacrificed for us." What did the Apostle Paul mean when he gave this strange title to the Lord Jesus? We must turn back to the Book of Exodus, and there we shall find the picture story or type to which he was referring.

As the years went by the children of Israel, the descendants of the seventy who came down to Egypt to live with Joseph, might be numbered by thousands, and at last the kings of Egypt began to fear that they would get too strong, and outnumber the Egyptians themselves; so they treated them harshly, made them slaves and worked them very hard. They had to toil all day long, under the burning sun and cloudless sky, making bricks, and dragging heavy stones for the buildings and monuments of the king. Cruel taskmasters stood over them and beat them unmercifully. (The very Pharaoh who oppressed them so much, carved his name on the obelisk which was brought to London from Egypt, and now stands on the Thames Embankment.)

The children of Israel at last cried to God ; they told Him how unhappy they were, and He heard them, as He always does.   He was really waiting for them to beg Him to deliver them. This part of their story (see 1 Cor. x. 11) is a type of the condition of every sinner who has not yet been delivered from the cruel bondage of sin and Satan.   Each one of us is born in slavery, and only God can set us free.

When the time drew near for them to be delivered God appeared to Moses, whom he had already fitted to be their leader, and told him to go to Pharaoh with a message.   " Let My people go," He said, but Pharaoh would do nothing of the sort.   He only made their bondage harder.   That is what Satan does now. When God is about to deliver anyone he tries to prevent it, for he wants to keep his slaves, and so he makes them more unhappy than ever.   God sent one trouble after another to Pharaoh and his people, but he only became more and more determined to resist God, until the last plague, the slaying of the firstborn, made him long to get rid of the children of Israel.

God said that on a certain night a destroying angel would pass through the land of Egypt and visit every house. It was to take place at midnight, and the eldest in every family would die suddenly. There was only one way of keeping the angel out, and every one who believed that God would do what He had said, took care to follow His directions, and then they were perfectly safe.

On the 10th day of the month, the father of each family was to go to the flocks and choose a perfect lamb and bring it home. For three days they watched it and cared for it, and then on the evening of the 14th day the lamb was to be killed, its blood put in a basin, and with a brush, made of a few sprigs of a certain little common plant that grew on the walls, he was to sprinkle the blood on the side-posts and above the door. No destroying angel could pass that precious blood, and every one in the house was safe, for God said : " When I see the blood I will pass over you."

That was what the Apostle Paul meant when he said : " Even Christ our Passover is sacrificed for us," for every one who trusts in Him is safe for ever.   He is our Passover Lamb.   To accept Him for our Saviour, to believe that He died in our stead, just as the little lamb died for the firstborn in every family of the children of Israel, is like sprinkling the blood on the houses in which we dwell.   There was a difference between the shed blood and the sprinkled blood. The Egyptians who might have looked on that evening and seen the lamb killed, would know that its blood had been shed ; but to believe in the sprinkled blood was to put it on the house for God's eye to rest upon.

Many people believe that the Lord Jesus Christ died on Calvary nearly 1900 years ago, but it has not made any difference to them.   They believe His blood was shed, but they have never believed on Him as their Saviour.   They have not with the hand of faith sprinkled the blood, and said : " He died for me."

The safety of the children of Israel depended entirely upon the blood.   It was not their feelings that made them secure.   In one house the family might have felt very frightened all night ; in another they might have been calm and confident.   But if the blood was on the door, both were equally safe.   If the blood was not there, neither palace guards nor prison walls could keep out the destroying angel.

In every house in Egypt there was one dead —either the firstborn or the lamb. If we had been able to look inside the house we should have been able to tell in every case which families had sprinkled the blood on their doors, by noticing how the people were dressed, and what they were eating for their supper. The children of Israel were dressed for a journey, for the next morning they were to leave Egypt for ever, and to start for the promised land. As they ate their supper their travelling shoes were on their feet, their loose garments were tied up ready to start ; and they had their staves at hand to help them to walk. They were eating roast lamb, for the lamb whose death had saved them was to be the food to strengthen them for the journey.

There was a very different scene that evening in the houses of the Egyptians who had not put the blood upon the doors. They were dressed in their ordinary garments ; they had put off their walking apparel, and as they were sitting at the supper table we should have seen them eating fish, cucumbers, melons, leeks, onions, and garlic. They were not feeding on the lamb! Thus we could have told that the blood was not upon the door. And so it is now. This is how we judge whether people are really Christians or not.

We cannot see into the hearts of those around us. We cannot tell if they are sheltered by the blood of the Lord Jesus, but we can tell their habits and their tastes, as represented by the food and the dress of the two classes of people in Egypt on that terrible night. When we see that anyone really loves the Bible, and is trying to please God, we may safely conclude that he or she has by faith taken shelter under the blood of the Lord Jesus. Can you say : " Even Christ my Passover was sacrificed for me " ?

A LONG JOURNEY

"Thou in Thy mercy hast led forth the people which Thou hast redeemed: Thou hast
guided them in Thy strength unto Thy holy
habitation."

Exodus 15:13

8

A LONG JOURNEY

ON the very morning after the Passover had been killed, and the blood of the lamb sprinkled on the doors, the children of Israel started on their journey to the Land of Promise. That night Pharaoh and his people were eager to get rid of them, and in every Egyptian home where the blood had not been sprinkled there were funeral preparations, "for the Egyptians buried all their firstborn" (Num. xxxiii. 4).

They were so busy with this that they allowed the Israelites to start. But Pharaoh very soon changed his mind. He did not want to lose his slaves, and with a great army he began to pursue. Satan never willingly gives up any of his servants.

It was on the third day that the children of Israel found themselves in a terrible position —the sea in front of them and Pharaoh's army behind.   They felt as though they were caught in a trap and there was no way of escape. But the God who had saved them, because they were sheltered by the blood of the lamb, was not going to leave them to their enemies.   He Himself was leading them in a wonderful way. As they journeyed, He went before in an upright cloud, shaped like a pillar.   During the night it shone like fire, so they were never in the dark.

When the Egyptians had almost caught the children of Israel, God came between the two hosts.   He moved the pillar of cloud so that instead of going in front of His people He went behind, and the pillar that was burning and shining on them was a wall of darkness to the Egyptians.   They pursued, but could not see where they were going, and probably had not the least idea that God had worked another great miracle.

He had opened a way right through the Red Sea.   The waters piled themselves up like two great walls, and the children of Israel marched on dry land between them, by the light of the pillar of fire.

On came the Egyptians, but they did not succeed in catching their late slaves.   It was pitch dark ahead and God made their chariot wheels come off so that there was the greatest confusion. Just as morning dawned and they found out where they were, God told Moses to stretch forth his rod over the sea and the waters returned to their place.

The Apostle Paul tells us that all these things were types. Because we who have believed are counted to have died with the Lord Jesus, we have been cut off for ever from the life of bondage. The old taskmasters, sin and Satan, cannot hold us, for as Moses taught each one of the children of Israel to sing that day on the shores of the Red Sea : " The Lord is become my salvation."

And now the journey through the wilderness had begun. It need not have taken a fortnight to reach the land that God had given to them ; but because they were so full of unbelief, and so often rebelled against God, it took them forty long years. It is because of our want of faith that we cannot enter into the blessings which God has given to us.

Some time ago I was taking a Bible-class at Mr. Moody's home in America, and I asked this question : " Can you tell me where it says,

' By faith the children of Israel wandered for forty years in the wilderness ' ? "

Quite a number in the class answered at once : " In the eleventh of Hebrews."

" Will you tell me the verse ? " I asked.

They turned over the leaves of their Bibles till they came to the chapter, and there was silence for a minute or two while they looked for the words ; but they could not find them in that chapter, nor anywhere else in the Bible. Ah no, as I reminded them, it was not " by faith," but because of unbelief that the children of Israel were kept so long out of their inheritance.

In spite of all their sinfulness God did not leave them.   He still guided them and never once took away the pillar of cloud and of fire. When we trust in the Lord Jesus, God's Holy Spirit takes up His abode in our heart.   Upon believing God puts His seal upon us by giving us His Spirit.   He says : " That one is Mine for ever."

Just as He never took away the pillar of cloud from Israel till they reached the Land, He never takes away the Holy Spirit from one who has trusted in Him.   " If any man have not the Spirit of Christ, he is none of His ; "

but having redeemed us by blood as on the Passover night, and delivered us by power as at the Red Sea, we are His to all eternity.

Sometimes the pillar stood still in their midst over the Tabernacle which God directed them to make ; and then they rested in their tents. But when they saw the pillar rising they knew what it meant ; they were to pack up their tents and start again. Perhaps the pillar of cloud that led the way hid the path ahead, but they had only to follow. God never made a mistake. So He leads His children now, a step at a time ; day by day He shows them where He would have them go, and even chooses the place where they shall pitch their tents (Deut. i. 33).

> *He went Himself before us in the way*
> *To search us out a place to pitch our tents :*
> *He never sent us forth to choose the spot,*
> *But did Himself select each halting place—*
> *'Twas not enough that He should indicate*
> *The road that we must take to reach the land*
> *Which He had promised as our heritage.*
>
> *Oh wondrous condescension ! Who but He*
> *Could know the valleys and the hills and plains,*

And tell the safest place for us to camp ?
The rocky ledge beneath the mountain's shade,
Where we could shelter from the coming blast;
The grassy plot beside the gentle stream,
Where we could find refreshment by the way.
He knew the storms or sunshine that would come,
And chose accordingly the camping place—
The very best for each in all the vale.

If He had let us find it for ourselves,
We should have made in.ium'rable mistakes,
But now, in looking back o'er all the route,
We see He always chose unerringly.
We should have pitched beside the river's bed
When floods were just about to sweep the vale,
We should have sheltered underneath the cliff
When heavy landslips were about to fall !

O foolish heart, that fears to trust His choice,
And longs to pitch thy tent on other soil !
It is enough that He should go before,
Whose eyes can see both dangers and delights—
The present aud the future—both alike
Are plain to Him.   To-morrow's sunshine gleams
Already through the dark clouds of to-day,
Which are not dark to Him, but only bright;
So do not fear to trust Him to select
The place where thou shouldst daily pitch thy tent.

WILDERNESS PROVISION

"They thirsted not when He led them through the deserts."

Isaiah 48:21a

9

WILDERNESS PROVISION

WE are not told all that happened to the children of Israel during the forty years' journeying through the wilderness, but everything that is mentioned has a hidden meaning. There is some teaching in it for us to-day.

Many of the incidents had to do with God's provision. The Lord Jesus said to His disciples : " Take no thought for your life, what ye shall eat or what ye shall drink . . . for your Heavenly Father knoweth that ye have need of all these things." God proved it in the history of Israel.

At one of their first stopping-places, Marah, they eagerly ran forward to drink of the water they saw there, but to their disappointment it was so bitter and brackish that it was impossible to drink it. The people murmured, but God in grace found a remedy, and told Moses to throw a certain tree into the water, and it was healed.

The only way in which bitter water can be made sweet is by the fountain being healed by God. The tree was a picture of the Lord Jesus, who is several times called the Branch. He can sweeten bitter waters (see p. 229).

About a month after they left Egypt the children of Israel began to suffer very much from hunger, and again they began to complain to Moses and his brother Aaron. They thought of the food they used to eat in Egypt, and, forgetting all about the hardships, the slavery and the taskmasters, wished themselves back there.

It must be very grieving to God when those who have been set free from the bondage of sin and Satan, and have become Christians, long for the old life and for the pleasures of sin. But again God found a way out of their difficulty by meeting the need. He knew how real a need it was, and so He opened the doors of heaven and rained down bread for them to eat. All that the people had to do was to go out morning by morning and pick it up for themselves off the ground. On the Sabbath day they found none, for they were to gather on the sixth day enough for two days.

This heavenly bread was called Manna, and day after day for the rest of the forty years, God caused enough to fall to supply the needs of all that great host of people. They prepared it in different ways, sometimes baking it into cakes which tasted as sweet as honey. There is a legend among the Jews that the flavour of the Manna was just what each person liked best.

We are not left to guess what the Manna represented. In John vi. the Lord Jesus Himself explains it. He told the people that the Manna was just a picture of Himself. He said : "I am the Living Bread which came down from heaven." The "doors of heaven" were opened by God, and He came down to this earth to be the food of hungry sinners (Ps. lxxviii. 23).

The bread that fed the Israelites kept them alive for a time, but they all died one by one ; if we feed on the Lord Jesus, He gives us a new life. He tells us also what feeding on Him means. "I am the Bread of Life : he that cometh to Me shall never hunger ; and he that believeth on Me shall never thirst." "Coming" and "believing," that is all ; and just as bread and water satisfy our hunger and our thirst, so He can satisfy our heart when it hungers and thirsts after Him.

The next need of the children of Israel was for water. Again they came to Moses with their complaints, instead of going direct to God ; but God provided for them, and actually brought water out of a most unlikely place—a rock on the mountain-side. He said He would stand on the top of the rock, and Moses was to stand below and strike it with his rod, the rod that had been used to work so many miracles in Egypt, and that had been stretched over the Red Sea not long before. When Moses struck the rock as he had been told, instantly the water flowed, rivers of water enough for all the people.

Here we have another type of the Lord Jesus and what we have through Him. "That Rock was Christ." We often sing "Rock of Ages cleft for me," and because He was smitten, the water has flowed down for us.

The water itself is a type of the Holy Spirit. After the Lord Jesus had died on the cross, and had been buried, and had risen again, He ascended into heaven, and then God was able to pour down the Holy Spirit, as He had promised. When the Holy Spirit was given at Pentecost

(Acts ii.), Peter said : " Therefore, being by the right hand of God exalted, and having received of the Father the promise of the Holy Ghost, He hath shed forth this which ye now see and hear."

Some years afterwards, when the children of Israel were nearing the end of their journeyings, they again wanted water. This time God told Moses to speak to the rock, and the waters would flow. But he got angry with the people, and smote it again. This was a wrong thing to do, for he was spoiling God's type.

God is particular about His pictures being quite correct in every detail, and to smite the rock a second time was like teaching that the Lord Jesus had to be smitten twice. We know that He died once for all on the cross, and will never have to die any more. When John saw Him in the glory from the island of Patmos, He said : " I am He that liveth and was dead, and behold, I am alive for evermore."

Because Moses had done this thing, God would not allow him to go into the promised land with the people. He was only able to look at the country from the top of a mountain on the borders of the land ; and as he gazed at the beautiful landscape he saw all that he had

lost.   He prayed very earnestly that he might
enter the land, but God silenced him, and said :
" Let it suffice thee ; speak no more unto Me
of this matter."

Long years afterwards Moses' prayer was
answered.   He stood on "that goodly mountain," the Mount of Transfiguration, and talked
with his Lord of " His decease which He should
accomplish at Jerusalem," the antitype of the
smiting of the rock.   Perhaps Moses had had
some vision of that wonderful scene which
prompted him to pray that he might "see that
goodly mountain " (Deut. iii. 25), and that
prayer was answered at last.

THE BRAZEN SERPENT

"As Moses lifted up the serpent in the wilderness, even so must the Son of Man be lifted up."

John 3:14a

10

THE BRAZEN SERPENT

WHEN the Lord was talking to Nicodemus, He referred to an incident in the history of the children of Israel that was a beautiful type of His own death. "As Moses lifted up the serpent in the wilderness, even so must the Son of Man be lifted up ; that whosoever believeth in Him should not perish, but have eternal life " (John iii. 14, 15).

The children of Israel had been complaining again, as they so often had done, in spite of God's goodness to them. They were tired of their bread, and thought nothing of the water He had provided. "The soul of the people was much discouraged because of the way" (Num. xxi. 4). This was sin, and it soon led to actual rebellion against Him. "The people spake against God, and against Moses." How often we forget that when we allow ourselves to become depressed and discontented so that rebellious thoughts come into our hearts, it is sin.

Because of the murmuring of the people, God sent a great number of serpents amongst them. Multitudes of the people were bitten, and those who were bitten died. A great cry went up to Moses, for they saw and owned their sin, and begged him to pray for them. When Moses did so, God heard, as He always does, and He told his servant to make a serpent of brass like those that had bitten the people, and to set it on a pole—high up so that all could see it. "And it shall come to pass, that EVERY ONE that is bitten, when he looketh upon it shall live." Moses made a serpent as quickly as he could, and set it up, so that those on the very outside of the camp could see it : "and it came to pass (just as God had said) that if a serpent had bitten ANY MAN, when he beheld the serpent of brass, he lived."

The remedy was very simple. They had to do something which was quite easy, even a child could do it : they had only to look. It was for "every man" and "any man," for every boy and for every girl ; all could be healed. And so it is now. Not one Israelite that looked at the serpent died from the serpent's bite ; and not one sinner that looks to the Lord Jesus can be lost.

The remedy took the form of that which had done the mischief. It was a serpent that bit them, and it was a brazen serpent that healed. "Sin when it is finished, bringeth forth death" (Jas. i. 15). "The wages of sin is death" (Rom. vi. 23). And so when God devised the plan by which He could give life, He "made Him (the Lord Jesus) to be sin for us" (2 Cor. v. 21).

We do not read that every one of the Israelites was bitten, but the Apostle Paul tells us that each of us, without exception, has been poisoned by the bite of sin—"that every mouth may be stopped, and all the world may become guilty before God. . . . For all have sinned and come short of the glory of God" (Rom. iii. 19, 23). And "the soul that sinneth it shall die." We shall die eternally if we do not make use of the remedy.

There must have been all sorts of different cases in the camp. Some of the people were badly bitten ; some had several bites ; others scarcely felt anything, for the bite was so slight that it caused little trouble ; but the poison had been introduced in each case, and would do its deadly work. The remedy was the same for all, a look at the serpent of brass healed the bad cases as well as the less severe, the old as well as the young.

The serpents managed to reach the very outskirts of the camp, and those afar off as well as those near the centre needed the remedy. That was why it was set upon a pole, high and lifted up : " Every man may see it ; man may behold it afar off" (Job xxxvi. 25). As a symbol of this, the Lord Jesus was lifted up on the cross. " As Moses lifted up the serpent in the wilderness, even so must the Son of man be lifted up."

It would not have done any good for Moses to go round from tent to tent prescribing various remedies. He had but one thing to do—to point to the serpent of brass ; and if, having looked for ourselves and been healed, we want to help others, this is what we can do—we can point to the One who was lifted up on the cross of Calvary.

It would have been no use for the bitten Israelites to bathe their wounds, or to put ointments or plasters on them, or to bandage them up ; but there are many who try to get rid of their sins in this way. They bathe their wounds with tears of repentance ; they put on the ointment of good works, or plasters of good resolutions, and bandage themselves with doing their best ; but the bites of sin get no better with this sort of treatment ; a look at the Crucified One is what they need, and all they need.

It would have been useless for anyone to go round telling bitten ones of the seriousness of their case, describing the symptoms and their danger, unless they had gone on to point to the brazen serpent. We can imagine how some of the Israelites, after they had been healed, would look around for others that had been bitten, would eagerly point to the pole with the serpent of brass upon it, and would raise them from the ground and turn their faces towards it, even if they were almost dying. The mothers would lift their children in their arms, and point the little bitten ones to the remedy, for even a child can look.

It was not necessary for any of them to understand how the healing took place. It seemed a most unlikely thing that a look could cure ; but the secret was that it was doing what God had told them to do—taking Him at His word. We cannot understand how looking to the Lord Jesus on the cross can save us to-day. He has said : " Look unto Me and be ye saved."

We take Him at His word.   We look, and we are healed.

The Israelites knew they were bitten ; they looked, and they knew they were healed. There was no presumption in one man saying to another : " I was badly bitten ; I am sure I should have died very soon, but I heard Moses' clear voice ring through the camp.   It was just in time, and as I caught sight of the brazen serpent lit up by the rays of God's sun, I felt immediately that something had happened and now I am cured."

Is it presumption for us to say, in the words of Isaiah liii. : " He was wounded for our transgressions, He was bruised for our iniquities . . . and with His stripes WE ARE HEALED " ?   Some people think it is presumption to say we know we are saved, but John tells us that " he that believeth on the Son of God hath the witness in himself : he that believeth not God hath made Him a liar ; because he believeth not the record that God gave of His Son " (1 John v. 10).

If one of the Israelites had said : " I have looked, but I do not believe I am healed," it would have been making God a liar, because he believed not the record that God gave of the brazen serpent.

It was not a question of feelings. A man might have heard what Moses had said, and have understood exactly what he had to do, but if he lay in his tent, and did not look, he might have gone on saying : " I don't feel any better," till he died. The feelings came after a bitten one was healed, just as in the case of the woman who touched the hem of Christ's garment, and "straightway . . . felt in her body that she was healed " (Mark v. 29).

We may be quite sure that those Israelites who really believed the message did not put off looking. They had seen many dying around them, and we cannot imagine them saying : " I know I am bitten ; I know the bite will cause me to die, and of course I mean to look some time ; but I will wait till to-morrow, it will be time enough then." And yet how many there are who are acting just like this. They mean to become Christians some time, but are waiting for " a more convenient season." " Behold, now is the accepted time."

And what about the after-life of those who have been healed ? Are they safe from henceforth from all attacks of other serpents ? Mr. Spurgeon once said : " The healthiest way of living where serpents swarm is never to take your eye off the brazen serpent at all." Those who have looked learn that their only safety is to keep looking to the Lord Jesus; for the serpent is an emblem in Scripture, not only of sin as in this story, but of Satan himself, "the old serpent" (Gen. iii. 1; Rev. xx. 2). He cannot touch those who are looking to Christ. God puts a hedge round them as in the case of Job. Satan complained of this hedge, for he could not reach his victim: "Hast Thou not made an hedge about him on every side?" (Job i. 10). But Job himself did not understand this, and he complained that he was "a man whom God hath hedged in" (chap. iii. 23). Our only safety is to walk in obedience in the road that God has planned for us; for "whoso breaketh an hedge, a serpent shall bite him" (Eccles. x. 8).

We read that after they had been healed from the bites of the fiery serpents the children of Israel pitched their tents "towards the sunrising." This is what the Thessalonians did, for no sooner had they "turned to God from idols" than they began "to wait for His Son from heaven, even Jesus which delivered us from the wrath to come."

GEMS
FROM THE LAW

"Open Thou mine eyes, that I may behold
wondrous things out of Thy Law."
Psalm 119:18

11

GEMS FROM THE LAW

HIDDEN away among the commandments of Moses there are many beautiful pictures. The laws he received were not a mere collection of rules for the conduct of the Israelites, interesting because they show the manners and customs of an ancient people.

The Apostle Paul shows very plainly that it is not by accident that we may discover a spiritual meaning behind them. They were given by God and recorded with the very purpose. He tells us, for instance, that even the laws about cattle were spoken "altogether for our sakes" (1 Cor. ix. 10). It was not merely that God was particular about the way cattle were treated, though He did require the Israelites to be kind to their beasts. There was much more in it.

He wished to teach that those who labour

for Him are not forgotten.   He Himself cares for their comfort and their needs.   Therefore in the days of Moses He commanded : "Thou shalt not muzzle the mouth of the ox that treadeth out the corn," so that in the days of Paul and ever after, those who were con- secrated to His service should labour "in hope"—whether they plough the fields of the Master or reap His corn.

In his Letter to the Galatians, Paul uses a very striking expression : "The Scripture foreseeing . . ." (Gal. iii. 8), as though it were a person who could look down the long vista of years and see the coming Saviour.   This is what the Divine Author could do.

In the same chapter Paul quotes the words of the law—"Cursed is every one that hangeth on a tree" (v. 13).   Why was that particular death condemned above all others ?   Why did it not say : "Cursed is everyone that is burned ; cursed is everyone that is beheaded"?   Was it not that "the Scripture foreseeing" the death that the Lord Jesus would die on the cross for us, specially singled out that particular form of death as most accursed, so that when He came to die He stooped to the most shameful of all deaths, "even the death of the cross"?

There are two pictures of Jesus Christ our Lord among the laws concerning death. One law referred to a murder, the other to cases of manslaughter.

The first is in Deut. xxi., and it represents God's great inquest over the death of His own Son, with His provision for removing the guilt of those who were responsible. If a dead body were found "lying in the field," and it was not known who had slain the man, the elders and judges of Israel were to be summoned, and they were to make a careful measurement to the nearest cities.

The city "next unto the slain man" was to be accounted guilty, and a heifer that had never borne the yoke was to be offered up. In the presence of the priests and judges, the elders of the city were to wash their hands over the dead heifer, and having proclaimed that they were innocent, were to pray: "Be merciful, O Lord, unto Thy people Israel, whom Thou hast redeemed, and lay not innocent blood unto Thy people of Israel's charge. And the blood shall be forgiven them."

The dead body of the Lord Jesus was one

day seen by God "lying in the field"—"the field is the world." Who was guilty? He took His measuring line, and Jerusalem was proved to be the city next to the slain man. Jerusalem was guilty of His death, but the inhabitants could not say : "Our hands have not shed this blood, neither have our eyes seen it." They did not pray : "Lay not innocent blood unto Thy people Israel's charge"; for in their blind ignorance of what it meant they cried : "His blood be on us and on our children."

But they were not the only ones who were guilty. Every one who can say : "He was wounded for my transgressions, He was bruised for my iniquities, the chastisement of my peace was upon Him," is thus applying the measuring line to himself, and saying : "I am the city next to Him. It was for me He died. I am guilty of His death. God be merciful to me, the sinner."

Here, too, we have the double type. He was not only the one found slain in the field, but He was the heifer whose death put away the guilt of the murder, so that the city next to Him was forgiven.

The other law picture is found in the directions concerning the Cities of Refuge.

When the children of Israel had taken possession of their inheritance, they were to set aside
six cities, three on either side of the Jordan,
so that one would be easily accessible from
every part of the land. These were to be
Cities of Refuge for a man who by accident
caused the death of another.

Supposing two men were cutting trees in
the forest, and by accident the axe of the
one flew from his hand and struck his companion on the head so that he died, the man
who had caused his death would, according to
law, have forfeited his life, for the previous law
said : "Whoso sheddeth man's blood, by man
shall his blood be shed." The next of kin to
the dead man might at once take his life, but
this provision of the Cities of Refuge met his
need.

As soon as he saw that his companion, it may
be his friend, was dead, he would at once flee
to the nearest of the Cities of Refuge. He
dare not tarry a moment, he dare not go home
to say good-bye to his wife and family, he must
start at once.

On and on he would run, and as the sun
went down he might have thought within
himself : "I really must rest. Surely it will

not matter if I take an hour's sleep in this wood. I don't think the avenger of blood has started yet, there is plenty of time." But no, he would not dare to do that. His one anxiety would be to reach the City of Refuge. At last he sees the city in the distance, and on he runs. The gate is wide open and he reaches it just in time. The avenger of blood is already in sight, but passing within the walls he is absolutely safe.

Over a certain church door stands a large panel picture of this scene made by that wonderful artist in clay, George Tinworth. The man-slayer is represented as stumbling exhausted through the open door, the door of mercy. The avenger of blood has nearly over-taken him, and, failing to reach him, throws an axe at him, the axe of "justice"; but it does not touch him, for it is caught in "the door of mercy."

There is a verse in the Epistle to the Hebrews which links our salvation to this type, and speaks of those who have fled for refuge to lay hold upon the hope set before us (Heb. vi. 18). We are like that swift runner. We have forfeited our life by sin, and our only hope is in the Refuge which God has provided.

There must be no delay. We must flee immediately to Him, for we know not how soon justice might overtake us.

But once we are within that place of shelter, death cannot touch us, justice is powerless for ever, for we are safe in Him. The manslayer was to remain in the City of Refuge till the death of the High Priest. While our Great High Priest lives we must remain within our City of Refuge ; and seeing that He dieth no more, we shall remain safe in Him to all eternity.

There is a very beautiful type story about the Lord Jesus in Exodus xxi.—the law concerning the Hebrew bond-servant. If a Hebrew had become a slave to one of his brethren, the law required that the master should set him free in the year of jubilee ; but if, during the time of his servitude, he had been given a wife and had had children born to him, these belonged to his master. If he went out free, he could not take them with him : " He shall go out by himself" ; but here is the beautiful picture of loving sacrifice : " If the servant shall plainly say, I love my master, my wife and my children, I will not go out free, then his master shall bring him unto the judges ; he shall also bring him to the door, or unto the doorpost, and his master shall bore his ear through with an awl ; and he shall serve him for ever."

The Lord Jesus Himself was the Hebrew bond-slave. "He made Himself of no reputation, and took upon Him the form of a servant." He was sold for thirty pieces of silver, the price of a slave (Ex. xxi. 32 ; Matt. xxvi. 15). He might have gone out free ; He could have returned to the glory without going to the cross ; but if He had done so, He could not have won His people for Himself. He would have had to "go out by Himself." But He said : "Except a corn of wheat fall into the ground and die, it abideth alone ; if it die, it bringeth forth much fruit." He did not wish to "abide alone," and so He suffered alone. He was the Anti-type of the Hebrew servant who said : "I love My Master, I love My wife and My children, I will not go out free," and so from love to them He became the willing servant for ever ; and He says : "Mine ears hast Thou opened," or "pierced" (Ps. xl. 6).

GOD'S DWELLING PLACE

"Let them make Me a sanctuary; that I may dwell among them."

Exodus 25:8

"The Word was made flesh and dwelt among us."

John 1:14a

12

GOD'S DWELLING PLACE

THE most wonderful of all the types are those which have to do with God's Dwelling-place amongst the children of Israel. Soon after He had brought them out of Egypt He told Moses that He wanted to come and live amongst the people. He took him up into Mount Sinai, and there showed him the pattern of a large Tent, and gave him full directions as to how He wished this Tent, or Tabernacle, to be made.

He told him what materials and colours were to be used. He described the furniture, and how each separate vessel was to be made. It was a wonderful thing that for the first time since sin entered into the world, in the Garden of Eden, God should actually come down to dwell amongst sinful men.

The Tabernacle was His great object-lesson to teach the children of Israel, and us through

them, that this was His wish ; and also that
there was only one way by which sinners could
draw near into His presence.　Every part of it
was a picture of the Lord Jesus, and His work
for sinners ; and this explains why God Himself
took such pains to plan it all.

The time was still far distant when He
would come down and dwell among men in
the person of His Son Jesus Christ (John i. 14),
and when Christ's work upon the cross would
open up a way of access to God (Heb. x. 20) ;
so in order to teach Israel about Him and His
work, He taught them how to make the
Tabernacle.

The tents of the children of Israel in the
wilderness were pitched on four sides of an
oblong enclosure (about 150 feet long by 75
feet broad, the cubit being reckoned as 18
inches), which was curtained round by linen
hangings 7½ feet high.　In the midst of this
enclosure stood a tent, square at the ends, but
three times as long as it was broad, supported
on three sides by golden boards.　This was
the Tabernacle.

Seen from the outside it was not attractive,
for the golden boards and beautiful curtains
were hidden by a covering of skins.　When

Barak, and the princes of Moab and Midian, looked down upon it they might have said : " There is no beauty in that tent that we should desire it " (see Isa. liii. 2) ; but viewed from the inside it was like a little golden palace with a roof of beautiful embroidery.

In the open court between the gate and the Tabernacle stood two objects, both made of copper or " brass."

The one near the gate ($7\frac{1}{2}$ feet square and $4\frac{1}{2}$ feet high) was THE BRAZEN ALTAR. It was the first thing that met the gaze of those who entered or even looked through that gate. If anyone wished to come to God, to " get right with God," that was the only way ; they must come to the altar, and the life of some spotless animal must there be offered. Its blood must be poured out, and the fire must consume it. The man had forfeited his life by sin—another life must be given instead. When the Israelite brought his burnt-offering or his sin-offering, before killing it he laid his hand upon the animal's head, and by so doing he became identified with it—the acceptableness of the perfect animal passed to the sinful man, and he was accepted : that was the teaching of the burnt-offering. Or the sin of the sinner passed to the spotless substitute, and he was forgiven: that was the teaching of the sin-offering.

Thus, in type, God teaches how those who have sinned may be accepted and forgiven. After many many animals had been offered on the brazen altar, and many many years had elapsed, a prophet of Israel was sent of God to make a great proclamation. John the Baptist saw approaching him a lowly Man known amongst men as "Jesus of Nazareth"; and John cried: "Behold the Lamb of God which taketh away the sin of the world" (John i. 29).

Some years ago a friend of mine wished to make a model of the Tabernacle. He studied and carried out as far as possible the directions in the Book of Exodus, and made everything exactly according to the measurements, but on a small scale. Much of the work he could do himself, but he had to get someone who was accustomed to working in metal to help him with the gold, silver, and copper.

The man he employed was a notoriously bad man though a skilful worker. My friend explained to him just what he wanted, and amongst other things sketched and described the "brazen" altar, and told him what it represented and what it taught. While the man made the little copper model ($2\frac{1}{2}$ inches square), he thought about what he had heard, he thought of his sins and of all the lambs that were once offered to God on Israel's altar, and then of the Lamb of God who died on the cross for sinners.

Before he had finished the model, he had accepted the Lord Jesus as his own Saviour. I have that model now, and when I show it, I delight to tell people how one man at least learnt through it how his sins could be put away.

Have you ever been to the brazen altar? Have you seen the Lamb of God dying on the cross for you? The Israelite who slew his offering and saw it laid on the altar, might have said: " It is wounded for my transgressions, it is bruised for my iniquities, the chastisement of my peace is upon it, and with its stripes I am healed—with its death I am forgiven." And when by faith we accept the Lord Jesus Christ as our Saviour, we too may apply to ourselves the beautiful language of Isaiah liii. 5, 6. No sin-offering has been required by God since then. The One to whom all the Jewish sacrifices pointed has died "according to the Scriptures "; has been raised again "according to the Scriptures" to show that God is satisfied; and He is even now sitting on God's right hand, alive for evermore.

The other object in the outer court was a large basin of water called THE LAVER. We do not know its size, nor how the water was taken out of it for use, but the high priest and his sons were to wash their hands and feet when they served God in the Tabernacle.

We are not left in doubt as to what this laver meant, for the Lord Jesus when He was on earth explained it. He knew all about the Tabernacle in the wilderness, for He was God Himself, the Jehovah, who in Old Testament days had spoken to Moses.

When He was with His disciples in the Upper Room, just before He died, He poured water into a basin and washed their feet (John xiii. 1–17). Then He explained that His act had a spiritual meaning. Their feet, their ways, must be cleansed that they might have part "with" Him in fellowship, communion, and service. It was not a washing for salvation, as He showed Peter when he impulsively exclaimed: "Lord, not my feet only, but also my hands and my head."

The laver was not for this ; " He that is washed needeth not save to wash his feet." It was not for regeneration, for the new birth, but in order that those who, like the sons of Aaron, had been born into the family, might come to God in worship with cleansed feet. Thus the laver and the altar tell us of God's twofold provision for cleansing. " Christ also loved the church, and gave Himself for it (on the altar) ; that He might sanctify and cleanse it with the washing of water by the Word " (in the laver). Eph. v. 25, 26.

The Tabernacle was divided into two parts —the outer chamber, called the Holy Place, and the innermost one, the Holiest of All. If a cubit really measured 18 inches, as is supposed, the Holy Place was 30 feet in length, and 15 feet wide, and the Holiest of All 15 feet square—quite a small room.

They were divided by the Vail, a square curtain of finely woven linen, embroidered in blue and purple and scarlet ; and as we are distinctly told in the New Testament, this Vail was itself a beautiful type of the Lord Jesus. Beyond the Vail, in the Holiest of All, God's presence dwelt, and was seen in the dazzlingly bright glory that filled the place, making it the most sacred spot on earth.

Only once a year was anyone allowed to enter, so we read in the Epistle to the Hebrews : "Into the second (Tabernacle) went the high priest alone once every year, the Holy Ghost this signifying, that the way into the Holiest of All was not yet made manifest" (Heb. ix. 7, 8). This is a very wonderful statement for it tells us that the square curtain called the Vail was placed in the Tabernacle by the Holy Spirit. He was the Architect, and by it He was teaching a great lesson.   It shows also that all the different parts of the Tabernacle must have been designed by Him, and it is not therefore fanciful for us to seek out their meaning.

While the Tabernacle had its standing, in the days before the Lord Jesus died, the way into God's presence was not revealed.   A verse in the next chapter of Hebrews tells us something more, for we learn that the Vail represented the flesh of the Lord Jesus, and that since He died we may draw near. "Having therefore, brethren, boldness to enter into the Holiest by the blood of Jesus ; by a new and living way which He hath consecrated for us, through the Vail, that is to say, His flesh ; . . . let us draw near " (Heb. x. 19–22).

So important was this truth that the Vail was not allowed to remain unrent one moment after the Lord died. As He expired it was rent in the Temple "from the top to the bottom "—not from the bottom to the top, for it was God's hand and not man's that rent it. It shows us how much God thinks of His types—He would not allow this one to be inaccurate even for a few minutes. Against the passages which tell of the rending of the Vail we might write, " The Holy Ghost this signifying, that the way into the Holiest of All IS NOW made manifest."

We read in Isaiah liii.: " It pleased the Lord to bruise Him." The type explains that wonderful statement. If we use this simile and say : " It pleased the Lord to rend the Vail," it becomes plain at once. At last the way is open, now there is access into God's presence. And we have not to enter " alone," as the priest of old did. He, who is our great High Priest as well as the Sacrifice for sin, is there to meet us, to welcome us, to intercede for us, and to answer for us.

Have *you* ever taken advantage of this opened way ?

Some people teach that the Lord Jesus merely lived and died as an example, but His life on earth would never have brought sinners to God. The Vail was set up to DIVIDE between the two parts of the Tabernacle (Ex. xxvi. 33), to keep man out from God's presence ; and His perfect life only shows how impossible it is for us to live according to all God's requirements. It was the RENT Vail that opened the way, and it was because the Lord Jesus DIED for sinners that we may draw near.

Within the Holiest of All stood THE ARK, another beautiful figure of the Lord Jesus. It was a small chest made of wood and overlaid with gold, and inside it were the tables of stone on which were inscribed God's Law. The first tables had been broken on account of Israel's sin (Ex. xxxii. 19), but here these were perfectly kept (Deut. x. 1–5). The Lord could say : "Thy Law is within My heart."

The lid of the Ark—THE MERCY-SEAT, was of pure gold ; and two cherubim, of one piece with it, bent over it with outstretched wings. THE BLOOD was sprinkled on the mercy-seat, and plentifully sprinkled on the ground in front of it, for when we approach into God's presence there is always the reminder for God and for us, that the Lord Jesus has died for us.

The Apostle Paul explains this part of the type, for he tells us that the Lord Jesus was set forth to be a mercy-seat: "Whom God hath fore-ordained to be a propitiatory or mercy-seat" (Rom. iii. 25, R.V., marg.). It was at the mercy-seat that God could meet the sinner, and it is in Christ that He can meet with us. It was God's throne, and we may do what even the high priests of old could not do. They entered with fear, but we may "come boldly to the throne of grace, that we may obtain mercy (for the past), and find grace (for the present and for the future) to help in time of need" (Heb. iv. 16).

In the outer Tabernacle, the Holy Place, there were three holy vessels at which Aaron and his sons ministered to God. These also spoke of Christ and His people. There was THE GOLDEN CANDLESTICK, shining for God; there was THE GOLDEN TABLE on which the twelve loaves lay before God, telling of Christ in the presence of God for us; there was THE GOLDEN ALTAR at which the sweet savour of Christ ascended to God. It all spoke of Christ

and it all told of God's delight in Him. The
priests could *see* the light, could *smell* the
incense, and *eat* the bread (after it had lain a
week on the table), but it was for God first.

There is no mention of the golden altar in
Hebrews ix. 2, where the contents of the Holy
Place are enumerated, for there is no need of it
since the Vail has been rent. We, who have
been saved by His grace, are called to be holy
priests unto God to offer spiritual sacrifices
(1 Pet. ii. 5), to offer the sweet savour of Christ
Himself to God, not in the outer place but in
the Holiest of All. We may bring our prayers,
our worship, in the Name of Him whose
"Name is as ointment poured forth," and offer
them at the throne of grace itself.

The brazen altar, the laver, and the Ark
were in a straight line, and every worshipper
must FIRST go to the altar.

Have *you* tried to offer worship to God
without coming to the altar—without knowing
that your sin has been put away ? He cannot
admit you to His presence thus, but if you will
accept the Lord Jesus as your Saviour, and His
work on the cross as the ground of your salvation, you are invited to come without fear into
God's own presence.

The most easterly point in the Tabernacle was the gateway by which the sinner entered with his sin upon him. The most westerly was the mercy-seat, the throne of God, and "as far as the east is from the west, so far hath He removed our transgressions from us." What an immeasurable distance between the place of an unforgiven sinner and the place of a pardoned one in the presence of God by faith! "At that time ye were without Christ, . . . having no hope, and without God in the world : but, now, in Christ Jesus ye who sometimes were far off, are made nigh by the blood of Christ. . . . For through Him we both (Jew and Gentile) have access by one Spirit unto the Father." And this place of privilege may be yours to-day, for it is accorded to all whose sins have been put away by the precious blood ; and thus you will be able to join in that song of praise : "Unto Him that loved us and washed us from our sins in His own blood, and hath made us kings and priests unto God and His Father, to Him be glory and dominion for ever and ever. Amen."

There is one incident in the life of Daniel which suggests the great sacredness of the vessels of the Tabernacle and Temple. When

Belshazzar, King of Babylon, made a feast for a thousand of his nobles, he covered the banqueting table with the golden vessels which had been taken by Nebuchadnezzar from the Temple at Jerusalem, and the golden candlestick helped to light up the gorgeous scene. God took notice of this, and " the fingers of a Man's hand " were seen writing the message of judgment on the wall just above the candlestick. The terrified King and his courtiers trembled as they saw the handwriting, though they could not understand its meaning till Daniel was sent for. The climax of his charge against the King was that he had brought the holy vessels, and that he and his lords, his wives, and his concubines had drunk from them. They were intended for God's use alone, and were polluted by the proud King. The candlestick which was meant for the Tabernacle alone, was being used to light up this worldly scene, and this was one great reason why the judgment fell. God intends His children to shine for Him, but if they allow themselves to be used by the world they too will be in danger of incurring His displeasure.

THE ARK
AND ITS HISTORY

"Thou shalt put the mercy-seat above upon the ark; . . . and there I will meet with thee, and I will commune with thee from above the mercy-seat."

Exodus 25:21,22a

13

THE ARK AND ITS HISTORY

THERE are several very interesting stories about the Ark, and each one is typical of something in the life, or character, or work of the Lord Jesus Christ. We have already seen that the Ark was a type of Himself in its construction and its place in the Holiest of All.

"IN THE MIDST."—All through the wilderness journeyings, from the days when the Tabernacle was first made, the Ark was in the middle of the encampment. This reminds us that the Lord Jesus should always be the centre round which His people gather—"Jesus in the midst."

GOING ON BEFORE.—On one occasion only, in the wilderness, the Ark was carried in front, to lead the way and to seek out a resting-place for them. It was as a rebuke to Moses for having suggested that they needed anyone but God to be to them "instead of eyes" (Num. x.

31, 33). This illustrates the truth that the Lord Himself is to be our Guide. The Good Shepherd goes before His sheep.

CROSSING THE JORDAN.—When the children of Israel were about to enter the land of promise, and had to cross the river Jordan, God commanded Joshua to speak to the priests whose duty it was to carry the Ark, and tell them to walk right into the river. The moment their feet touched the water the river divided in front of them.

The golden Ark could not be seen for it was covered with skins, and over them was a cloth of blue. But the people could all see this blue object as they marched past it in the bed of the river. When every one of them had passed over safely, without even wetting their feet, the priests carrying the Ark came out of the river, and the waters flowed on again once more.

This story is a type of the Lord Jesus going down into the river of death for us, and by His death making a way for us into all the blessings God has promised for His people. He is the First and the Last, the Author and Finisher of faith. When He was on earth the gold could seldom be seen, but the blue, the heavenly, was always visible. He was always the heavenly Man.

We often sing hymns about Canaan, as though the promised land were a type of heaven ; but there will be no fighting in heaven, and the children of Israel had to do a great deal of fighting before they could really come into possession of what was theirs by promise.

We are told by the Apostle Paul that we who have trusted in the Lord Jesus Christ are "blessed with all spiritual blessings in heavenly places in Christ" (Eph. i. 3). Our inheritance is not on earth, but we must take possession by faith of all the precious things which He gives to us.

I once stayed at a beautiful place in Scotland. The property had passed into the hands of our host when he was a little boy of four years old, and one day soon afterwards he was taken to see it. Half the county belonged to him, but he did not know it ; and so as he was walking through the lovely gardens with his nurse he turned to her and said : " May I pick a flower ? " There are some Christians who are very like this. They do not know how rich they are. In fact none of us really understands fully, for the riches of Christ are unsearchable.

THE TAKING OF JERICHO.—The taking of Jericho is the next picture.   The Apostle Paul says in 2 Cor. x. 4, 5, that " the weapons of our warfare are not carnal (that is, not guns and swords), but mighty through God to the pulling down of strongholds."   He must have been thinking of the day when the walls of Jericho fell.

It was a strongly fortified place not far from the Jordan.   How could the children of Israel have taken it, unless God had given it into their hands ?   Day after day the people marched round the city, once a day for six days, and seven times on the seventh.   What a strange procession it was !   Seven priests blowing trumpets, and others in the centre carrying the blue-covered Ark, while armed men went in front and followed.   Silently they marched, for they were not to shout till they compassed it the thirteenth time.   And then the walls fell, so that the armed men were able to go straight up through the breaches in front of them, and thus take the city.

The meaning of the name Jericho is, we are told, " fragrant with spices," and it may represent the attractions of the world which are so often spread before the young Christian when he has crossed over Jordan by faith and stands in the land.

We are not commanded to fight against the world, but to carry Christ with us against the temptation, and we shall then gain the victory, as the children of Israel did when they carried the Ark round Jericho. John says: " Whatsoever is born of God overcometh the world ; and this is the victory that overcometh the world, even our faith " (1 John v. 4).

IN THE HANDS OF THE PHILISTINES.—In 1 Sam. iv. we have a description of the Ark falling into the hands of the Philistines. "The Ark of God was taken." This incident in its history reminds us of the time when our Lord permitted Himself to be taken in the Garden of Gethsemane. "Then took they Him" (Luke xxii. 54). The Ark was captured because God had "delivered His Strength into captivity and His Glory into the enemy's hand " (Ps. lxxviii. 60–62). Without God's permission the Philistines would have had no power to take it ; nor would the Roman soldiers have been able to take the Lord Jesus. With equal truth it might have been said on both occasions :

"Thou couldest have no power at all against Me except it were given thee from above" (John xix. 11) ; and "Him, being delivered by the determinate counsel and foreknowledge of God, ye have taken" (Acts ii. 23).

In the Temple of Dagon.—The Ark was carried into the temple of Dagon to celebrate the triumph of the god whom its captors worshipped ; but in the time of its seeming defeat and weakness it showed itself stronger than Dagon. After our Lord had allowed Himself to be taken He went down into death, into the domain of him who had the power of death, but though His heel was bruised He crushed the serpent's head (Gen. iii. 15).

The idol fell when God's Ark was placed in the temple ; and so when Christ comes into the heart the idols fall. This is very different from what the hymn says :—

" . . . I have all my idols torn
    From my heart, and now He keeps me by His power."

It is His presence alone that can do it. As in the parable, the strong man armed may keep his palace, but when the Stronger than he comes in, He overcomes him. We are not able to turn out the strong man, or to tear down the idols.

When in the garden the chief priests and Pharisees came to take Him, He had only to proclaim His Name, " I am," and " they went backward and fell to the ground " ; showing that the same Divine power dwelt in Him as in the Ark of old when it made the idol fall.

It is remarkable that the Ark was three days in the temple of Dagon (1 Sam. v. 2–4). On two succeeding " morrows " we read that the idol lay on the ground before it, and on the second morning it was broken in pieces. It is not likely that it was kept there any longer. So here we have another point in the type. We cannot doubt that as Jonah's " three days and three nights " inside the whale were a type of the " three days and three nights " spent by the Lord Himself " in the heart of the earth " (Matt. xii. 40), so also were the three days spent by the Ark in the house of the fish-god.

IN THE LAND OF THE PHILISTINES.—There was sorrow in the homes of the Philistines during the seven months that the Ark was in their land, for the hand of God was heavy upon them. After it had shown itself stronger than Dagon in the temple in Ashdod, it brought death and destruction upon the people themselves. Many were stricken with disease, and many died, so that they felt that they must get rid of the Ark. It was next carried to Gath and Ekron, and even heavier judgments fell on the people of those cities, so that they, too, were anxious to send it away.

In each city the number of deaths increased and the plagues grew worse, till at last the Philistines determined to get rid of the Ark altogether. They had boasted that they had taken possession of the God of Israel, but when they felt His power they no longer wanted to keep the symbol of His presence in their midst ; just as we read in the Gospels that the men of Gadara, when they had seen the power of the Lord Jesus, and when they had lost their herd of swine, begged Him to depart out of their coasts (Mark v. 16, 17).

The Philistines put the Ark upon a new cart drawn by cattle, and they watched to see if the cattle would carry it back to the land of Israel. Without taking a single wrong turning, and without any human guide to tell them the way, they bore it straight across the border to Bethshemesh.

THE MEN OF BETHSHEMESH.—The men of

the town were in the fields reaping, and when they saw the Ark coming they were glad, for all Israel had mourned because it had fallen into the hands of the Philistines. They lifted it off the cart and put it on a large stone in one of their fields, and then they broke up the cart, lit a fire with it, and sacrificed the cattle to God. But the men of Bethshemesh made a great mistake by looking into the Ark. They lifted off the mercy-seat, and uncovered the tables of the law. This was one of the very things that God had forbidden. The Ark was so holy that He would not allow it, and a great many of the men of Bethshemesh died because of their sin.

Here again the Ark is a type of the Lord Jesus. We must always remember that He is God as well as man, and we must be very reverent when we speak of Him. "No man knoweth the Son but the Father;" and the mystery of His Incarnation and Godhead is one into which we must not try to examine too closely. The attempt to define between the deity and the human nature of the Lord Jesus is like prying into the Ark, and has often led men astray. The men of Bethshemesh, like the Philistines, were eager to get rid of the

Ark, and they sent to a neighbouring town, Kirjath-jearim, begging that it should be fetched. So it was carried to the house of Abinadab, a Levite, and it remained with him for twenty years.

DAVID AND THE ARK.—When David came to the throne he remembered the Ark, and could not rest till he had brought it to Jerusalem. But another very sad thing happened before this was successfully accomplished. God had commanded that when the Ark was carried from place to place it should be borne on the shoulders of the Levites, but David forgot this command, and thought he would copy the Philistines. He had heard about the new cart they had used, and how God had guided the cattle, and he decided that this was a very good way of carrying it (2 Sam. vi.).

The procession started from the house of Abinadab with great rejoicings ; David with all the people accompanied it, the Levites playing on all sorts of instruments of music, and Abinadab's sons walked by the side of the cart. But the road was rough, and suddenly one of the cattle stumbled and shook the cart, so that Uzzah, the son of Abinadab, was afraid that the Ark would fall. He put out his hand

and took hold of it, and instantly he fell dead beside it.

God had commanded that no man should touch the Ark, and it was not necessary when it was carried as He had directed, by means of the staves. It must have been a terrible moment for David when he realised what he had done. The Philistines knew nothing about the "due order," but David knew (1 Chron. xv. 13) ; and by copying the Philistines he brought this trouble upon his people. This has often happened since in the history of the Church ; for it was by copying the methods of paganism that Christianity so quickly became corrupted.

It was sad that the son of Abinadab, in whose house the Ark had rested so long, should thus have fallen. It had been in Uzzah's home for so many years that perhaps it had lost its sacredness to him. This, alas, has but too often been repeated in homes which have received great blessing from the presence of the Lord in their midst.

The death of Uzzah made David relinquish his purpose for a time, for he was greatly afraid at this manifestation of God's power and majesty, and was like Peter when he cried:

"Depart from me, for I am a sinful man, O Lord."

THE HOUSE OF OBED-EDOM—The Ark was not carried back to the house of Abinadab, but was taken to that of Obed-edom ; and by and by the news of the abundant blessing that had visited this house made David determine once more to bring it to Jerusalem. Amid songs of gladness it was carried on the shoulders of the Levites, and placed in the tent which David had prepared for it.

Several of these incidents in the history of the Ark furnish us with a wonderful illustration of the truth of 2 Cor. ii. 15, 16 : " We are unto God a sweet savour of Christ, in them that are saved, and in them that perish ; to the one we are the savour of death unto death, and to the other the savour of life unto life."

During the seven months that it remained in the land of the Philistines the Ark brought nothing but death and destruction. What a contrast to the history of its sojourn in the house of Obed-edom, where it brought nothing but blessing ! To the Philistines it was " the savour of death unto death " ; and to the house of Obed-edom, " the savour of life unto life." "All that pertained to him" came in for a share of the blessing ; and it was noised abroad so that the king heard of it.

So will it be with one in whose heart the Lord has made His abode—others will hear of it, and will want to have the same blessing. Here the type fails, for Obed-edom had to lose the Ark from his house when David took it to Jerusalem, though we do not hear that he lost the blessing. "We will come unto him and make Our abode with him," is the promise to each one who loves the Lord Jesus and keeps His words ; and if others gain the blessing through us we shall not be the losers.

The 24th Psalm is generally supposed to have been sung on this occasion : "Lift up your heads, O ye gates ; . . . and the King of glory shall come in."

But the return of the Ark was a type of the return of the Lord Jesus after His victory over Satan and death, and so the Psalm is also beautifully applicable to the ascension and to the welcome He, as the returning Conqueror, received from the angelic choirs.

They crowd the golden ramparts, and eager earthward peer,
The Victor is returning, and quickly will appear,
Lift up your heads, ye portals, with joyful note they sing,
The everlasting gateways with angel echoes ring.

" The King of Glory cometh ; oh, open wide the gate ! "
And then the royal challenge, the answ'ring choirs await;
"Who is this King of Glory ? oh, answer, who is He ?
His hands and feet are wounded, the nail-prints we can see."
" Jehovah strong and mighty, the Victor in the fight,
He is the King of Glory, and His the throne by right ;
He now to heaven returneth—His earthly race is run,
The enemy is vanquished, the battle has been won."

The 24th Psalm may also have been sung by the united choirs when the Ark was placed in the Temple by Solomon : a wonderful picture of the time when the " holy temple unto the Lord " will be complete, and all the redeemed will take their places round Himself (p. 199). If the first question and answer in Psalm xxiv. 8 are applicable to the ascension, the second, in verse 10, are equally appropriate to His return to Heaven with His people.

Once more the angel myriads are thronging round the
   gates,
Once more all heaven is joyful, a mighty welcome waits,
" Lift up your heads ye portals," in eager haste they sing,
The everlasting gateways again with echoes ring.
" The King of Glory cometh ; oh, open wide the door ! "
" Who is this King of Glory ? " the challenge comes once
   more ;
" The King, the King of Glory, as Lord of Hosts has come,
Not now alone returning, He brings His people home."

DAVID AND GOLIATH

"So David prevailed over the Philistine with
a sling and a stone, and smote the Philistine,
and slew him; . . . and took his sword, and
drew it out of the sheath thereof, and cut off
his head therewith."

1 Samuel 17:50,51

14

DAVID AND GOLIATH

IN studying the history of the Ark we have already touched upon some incidents in the life of David, but he is himself in many ways a beautiful type of the Lord Jesus, as the anointed king, the good shepherd, the victorious deliverer, the faithful friend, the rejected one who waits for his crowning day, the great leader, the gracious king, and the one who makes preparation for the building of a magnificent temple.

It was not long after the death of Joshua that the children of Israel began to wish to be like the nations around them. They wanted to have a king of their own, but this was not God's plan for them at the time. He was their King, and He wished to remain their one Ruler. But He let them have their desire, and the first king seemed just the one to be the leader of the nation. He was such a fine handsome

man, head and shoulders taller than anyone
else !

He reigned for forty years, but though God
often allowed the Israelites to be victorious over
their enemies, Saul was not a success. He
filled up the ranks of his army with all the
finest men in Israel, but when they had to fight
against the Philistines he did not inspire them
with confidence, and they " trembled after him "
(1 Sam. xiii. 7).   On several occasions he disobeyed God, who determined to choose a king
" after His own heart."

This time the choice was not according to
the outward appearance.   God looked at the
heart, so He sent His servant Samuel the prophet
to Bethlehem, and told him to anoint one of
the sons of a man named Jesse.

One by one they stood before Samuel, and
as he looked at them God whispered again and
again in his ear : " No, not this one, this is not
he."   At last seven sons had all passed before
Samuel, and he asked their father if he had no
other son.   " Yes," said Jesse, " there is one
more, but he is only a lad, and he is looking
after the sheep."   " Send and fetch him," said
Samuel.   So David the shepherd boy was sent
for, and directly the prophet saw him he knew

that this was the chosen of God, and he anointed him before them all.

God had watched David when he had been all alone with the sheep on the hillside, and he had listened when he was singing songs of praise and playing skilfully on his harp. Perhaps it was in those shepherd days that David first composed the 23rd Psalm, and sang: "The Lord is my Shepherd"; or that he watched the stars in the cloudless sky, and sang: "The heavens declare the glory of God, and the firmament showeth His handiwork."

The anointing of David at Bethlehem reminds us of the time when the Lord Jesus at His baptism was anointed by the Holy Spirit, who descended upon Him in the form of a dove, and a voice out of heaven said: "This is My beloved Son, in whom I am well pleased." God thus proclaimed that the Lord Jesus was the promised Messiah, the One who would reign upon the throne of David as King of Israel, but in both cases the time had not yet come for God's Anointed to reign.

In the next chapter (1 Sam. xvii.) we read the beautiful story of how David met in single combat Goliath, the great enemy of Israel, and in the Gospels we read how the Lord Jesus, immediately after His baptism, was led by the Spirit into the wilderness, that He might fight and conquer Satan, the great enemy of His people.

The two armies were encamped on the mountain-side with a valley between them. In those days there were no cannon, and it was quite safe for them to pitch their tents within sight of one another. They did not need to dig trenches in which to hide.

As they were waiting for the battle, there came out from the camp of the Philistines a great giant, more than nine feet high, fully armed with helmet of brass and coat of mail, a very terrifying figure. He stood in the valley, and proclaimed in a loud voice, so that the Israelites all along the mountain-side could hear, that he was ready to do battle with anyone they would send out to fight him.

The Israelites were very much alarmed, for this continued for forty days, reminding us that the Lord Jesus was forty days in the desert tempted of the devil. Every day Goliath came out and shouted his challenge. But there was no one to take it up. Even Saul himself, Israel's chosen king, was no good at all.

One day Jesse sent his son David with a

present to some of his soldier brothers who
were in the army of Saul, and while he was
talking with them Goliath's loud voice was
heard. David asked what it meant, and made
many inquiries as to what would be the reward
of the man who slew the giant. His words
were repeated to Saul, and David was quickly
brought before the king. When he offered
to go out and fight the giant, Saul warned
him, and thought he had undertaken a hopeless
task ; but he was really very glad that someone
should try and silence the Philistine.

David knew where to look for help, and he
told Saul how God had enabled him to overcome both a lion and a bear that had attacked
one of the lambs of his flock. Here we have a
beautiful type of the Good Shepherd. David
would not allow the lion to have one of his
sheep, but risked his own life to save it. But
the type fails, for the Lord Jesus, the Good
Shepherd, had to do more than RISK His life,
He GAVE it for the sheep (John x. 11).

Saul was very anxious to array David in his
own armour, and he was obliged to submit to
it being tried on, but it was soon off again.
He did not want Saul's helmet of brass ; God
would cover his head in the day of battle

(Psalm cxl. 7) ; he wanted no shield, for he could say : " Thou hast given me the shield of Thy salvation." He knew that God is "a buckler to all those that trust in Him " (Psalm xviii. 30, 35).

And so he went out to meet the giant with his shepherd's sling and five smooth stones from the brook. The scrip or bag into which he placed them had often done service before, when he tended his father's sheep in the fields of Bethlehem. In it he would carry food for himself, and remedies for sick and wounded sheep, but now he put into it stones for the enemy.

When our Lord went forth as His people's Champion to meet their great enemy in single combat, His weapon was the Word of God. " It is written " was hurled again and again at the tempter as He quoted three times from the Book of Deuteronomy. The verses we learn from the Bible may prove the very weapon with which we may be able to defeat the foe. If we store our memory and our heart with God's Word, we find many uses for it. We shall be able to feed on it ourselves, give help to others, and have stones ready for the enemy.

How eagerly the armies must have watched the two champions as they went forth to meet one another, the great Philistine giant and the young shepherd. The God whom Goliath defied guided the hand of David, and the stone from his sling hit Goliath on the temple, so that he fell on his face to the ground ; and with Goliath's own sword David cut off his head.

The Lord Jesus overcame Satan during the temptation in the wilderness, and in His death He finally vanquished him. He went to the cross that " through death (Satan's own sword) He might destroy him that had the power of death, that is, the devil " (Heb. ii. 14). And probably this took place over the very spot where the head of Goliath lay buried.

We read that David carried it to Jerusalem (1 Sam. xvii. 54) ; here it would be buried and a mound raised over it, and it is supposed that the name given to this hill was gradually changed from Galgoliath to Golgatha, " the place of a skull "—the skull of Israel's great enemy in the time of David. Was it not wonderfully appropriate that the " green hill far away " that had so long commemorated the victory of David, should be the place where

David's greater Son conquered a far greater enemy, crushed his head (Gen. iii. 15), and wrought a far more important deliverance than David had done?

DAVID
AND HIS FOLLOWERS

"Every one that was in distress, ... and every one that was discontented, gathered themselves unto him; and he became a captain over them."

1 Samuel 22:2

15

DAVID AND HIS FOLLOWERS

AFTER David had killed the giant Goliath, he led the army of Israel in pursuit of the Philistines ; and when they returned victorious from the slaughter, David became the hero of all the people. With music, and dancing, and songs of praise, they welcomed him home and celebrated his victory. But King Saul became very angry at this, for he did not like to hear all these notes of triumph ; and he grew more and more jealous when David's exploits were compared with his own. Though he gave him a place at court, and a command in the army, hatred was in Saul's heart.

But his eldest son, Prince Jonathan, was full of admiration and affection for David. "The soul of Jonathan was knit with the soul of David ; and Jonathan loved him as his own soul." He "delighted much in David"

(1 Sam. xviii. 1 ; xix. 2) ; and David loved him too, for long afterwards, at the death of Jonathan, he sang a lamentation over him and said : " Very pleasant hast thou been unto me : thy love to me was wonderful " (2 Sam. i. 26).

Jonathan realised that the Lord had " wrought a great salvation " through David (1 Sam. xix. 5), and so his heart was drawn towards his deliverer. It is when we see what the Lord Jesus has done for us, when we understand that He has wrought a far greater deliverance than David wrought for Israel, that we begin to love Him, and long to give Him the first place in our lives. This is " very pleasant " to Him.

Jonathan was quite willing for David to take the throne, and he gave him his most precious possessions. The Philistines had previously forced the children of Israel to give up all their swords, and only two remained in all the land. These two belonged to Saul and Jonathan, but Jonathan loved David so much that he was glad to give even this precious sword to him.

When Saul saw how much his own son loved David, he hated him still more, and tried to kill David, and even Jonathan as well, because

he stood up for David.   On two occasions Saul
threw his spear at David, but

> "Not a single shaft can hit,
>   Till the God of love see fit;"

and Saul had no power to do him any harm,
for "the Lord was with him."

At last David saw that it would be better
for him to leave the court, and he went about
from place to place hiding from Saul.   In the
First Book of Samuel we have an account of
some of his narrow escapes, for Saul pursued
him, and tried to get his people to betray him
into his hands.

In the days when David used to feed his
father's flock in the fields of Bethlehem, he
learned to know many a safe hiding-place, and
probably he had long known the Cave of
Adullam.   Here he took up his abode for a
time, and when the news spread, his family and
a number of men joined him.   They were the
beginnings of his army.

Some of them were strange recruits, for this
is how they are described: "Every one that
was in distress, and every one that was in
debt, and every one that was discontented
gathered themselves unto him; and he became

a captain over them " (1 Sam. xxii. 2). He
did not turn away any of them, for each one
was welcome. There was no standard of size,
they had to pass no medical examination.

David in the Cave of Adullam, receiving all
these strange recruits, is a beautiful type of the
Lord Jesus, for these are just the sorts of people
who flock to Him. It is these things that
make them want to come—distress, debt, and
discontent. How many come to the Lord Jesus
because they are in sore trouble ! Others feel
the weight of their sins, they know that they
owe a great debt to God which they can never
pay ; and when they come they find that He
welcomes them, heals their sorrows and pays
their debt.

But some who came to David were only
discontented ; they had not any great trouble,
yet they were not happy. The Lord Jesus does
not say that He will only receive us when
we are very sorry for our sins, when we are
in great distress. He wants us to come to Him
just as we are, if we have ever such a faint desire
for Him, just a feeling of discontent, a longing
for rest and satisfaction.

Some people stay away because they think
they do not feel sorry enough for their sins,

they think that they do not repent enough ; but David received those who were discontented as well as those who were in distress. The Lord Jesus says : " If any man thirst (and this includes boys and girls) let him come unto Me and drink " ; and the last invitation in the Bible is : " Whosoever will, let him take the water of life freely."

The 34th Psalm was composed at this time, and it greatly adds to its interest when we think of the character of David's audience in the Cave of Adullam. At first about four hundred men came to him there, but we read in 1 Chronicles xii. that many others joined them, " until it was a great host, like the host of God " (v. 22).

We hear nothing now about distress, debts, and discontent ! Intercourse with David and the training he gave them has changed the first recruits into veteran soldiers, and the others who come to him to the hold are the pick of the nation. The description is wonderfully varied, and suggestive. Some excelled in the use of the bow, others could hurl stones with either the right or the left hand. They were " men of war fit for the battle, that could handle shield and buckler, whose faces were like the faces of lions, and were as swift as the roes upon the mountains" (*v.* 8). And all these learned to " keep rank " with one another.

Those who enlist in the army of the Lord need these same characteristics. They have to meet the enemy in very different engagements, they have to use divers weapons of war (see Eph. vi. 10, 18) ; and it is very important that all should learn to keep rank. There was one characteristic which marked all David's followers : " they came with perfect heart " or " one heart to make David king." He was the centre of attraction, and they wanted " to help him." Have you joined the army yet ?

THE MAN WHO
CHANGED MASTERS

"They found an Egyptian in the field, and brought him to David."

1 Samuel 30:11a

"Being then made free from sin, ye became the servants of righteousness."

Romans 6:18

16

THE MAN WHO
CHANGED MASTERS

A FTER escaping from Saul many times, David and his little band of followers took refuge over the border of Israel in the land of the Philistines ; and the king gave David the city of Ziklag as his headquarters. Many of the Philistines did not approve of this, for they thought that the man who had slain their champion, Goliath, was not likely to be much help to them. They were right, for David and his men used to go out secretly into the country round and totally destroy villages and hamlets. But one day, while the little expeditionary force was absent from Ziklag, another enemy appeared on the scene. The Amalekites swept down upon the city, destroyed it with fire, and took away captive all the women and children.

When David and his men returned to find the city in ruins, and all their wives and sons and daughters gone, they were in great grief, and the men were quite inclined to blame David for the disaster. They even spoke of stoning him, but : " David encouraged himself in the Lord his God."

He knew where to go when in trouble, and he was not disappointed. He told God all about it, and asked Him what he had better do. He had learnt the great secret that we may go to God in prayer about the things that concern our daily life, and that of our dear ones, and so he definitely asked God two things : (1) " Shall I pursue after this troop ? (2) Shall I overtake them ? "

In those days God used to flash forth an answer in clearly understood words, and He not only replied to David's two questions, but added something more. This is still His way, for though we do not hear the words of the answers to our prayers, He gives "exceeding abundantly above all that we ask or think." His answer to David was (1) " Pursue ; (2) for thou shalt surely overtake them ; (3) and without fail recover all " (v. 8).

And so the little band started on their pursuit. They had not gone very far when they came upon a young man lying in a field almost dying,

and we read : " They brought him to David."
He was nearly starving, so before questioning
him they gave him something to eat and drink,
not only bread and water, but figs and raisins
as well. He soon revived and was able to give
an account of himself.

He had taken part in the burning of Ziklag,
for he was a servant to one of the Amalekites.
He himself was an Egyptian, but he had been
serving a very bad master who cared nothing
for him, for when he fell ill his master left him
by the wayside to die. He had been doing all
he could to injure David, but how kindly David
treated him ! He was willing to take him into
his service then and there.

This young Egyptian is just a picture of
every unsaved sinner. Sin and Satan are hard
masters. " But God commendeth His love
toward us, in that, while we were yet sinners,
Christ died for us " ; when we were " without
strength " and even " when we were enemies "
(Romans v. 6, 8, 10).

Before this young Egyptian took service
with David, there was one thing he wanted to
know. Would David not only promise to spare
his life but swear to him that his old master
should not get hold of him again ? He wanted

to have done with the Amalekite for ever. When we come to the Lord Jesus, we too change masters. He sets us free from the old master, and this is what we read in Romans vi.

It helps us to understand this chapter if we apply it first to the young Egyptian who was servant to the Amalekite. The Amalekites in Scripture are a type of our sinful nature, " the flesh " as it is called. Let us imagine that the Apostle Paul is here talking to that young Egyptian. He would have said something like this (compare Romans vi.)

Ver. 11. " Count yourself to have done with the old master who left you to die ; but re-member that you are alive through David who saved your life.

Ver. 12. " Let not the Amalekite have anything more to say to you, that you should obey him, for he has no right over you any more.

Ver. 13. " Neither use your strength in his service any longer, but yield yourself to David and serve him. . . .

Ver. 16. " Do you not know that you are the servant of the one you obey, whether the Amalekite or David ?

Ver. 17. " But God be thanked, though you

were the servant of an Amalekite, now you are one of David's men.

Ver. 18. "Being then made free from the old master you have become the servant of David.

Ver. 19. "As you were an obedient servant to the bad master in the past, and did all you could to injure David and his followers, now you must be a good servant to David, and do just what he tells you.

Ver. 20. "For when you served the Amalekite you did not belong to David.

Ver. 21. "What did you gain by the burning of Ziklag, and all the other things you are so ashamed of now?—it very nearly brought you to death.

Ver. 22. "But now being made free for ever from the old master, you have entered the service of God's chosen king, and his service will bring nothing but reward. He will never tell you to do anything of which you will have to be ashamed."

The story goes on to show how the young Egyptian was really able to help David. He led the little band to the camp of the enemy, and they were able to overcome them and to recover all the captives that had been taken at the burning of Ziklag.   "And David recovered all."

If there is anyone who reads this story who has not yet entered the service of the Lord Jesus, will you not do so to-day ?   Do not wait till the old master has starved you, leave him at once.   You do not need to give a month's notice.

And when you enter the service of the Lord Jesus, the old masters, sin and Satan, will have no right to you any more.   How wonderful it is that the Lord Jesus not only forgives us for what we have done when we were His enemies, but takes us into His service, and allows us to help Him in His work.

DAVID
AND MEPHIBOSHETH

"David said unto him, Fear not: for I will surely shew thee kindness for Jonathan thy father's sake, ... and thou shalt eat bread at my table continually."

2 Samuel 9:7

17

DAVID AND MEPHIBOSHETH

WHEN David came to the throne he did not forget his love for Jonathan his friend, and after he had been reigning for some time he began to look round and inquire if there were any of his family left that he could be kind to for Jonathan's sake. Yes, he was told, there was one, but he lived a long way off at Lodebar. This was poor lame Mephibosheth.

When the news of Saul and Jonathan's death came to their household there was great alarm, and the nurse of Mephibosheth fled with him in her arms, for he was only five years old. But in their haste he fell, and was so badly hurt that he was lamed for life. Now he was a grown man, but he had never dared to come back for fear of David.

He probably thought that as he was a grandson of King Saul, David might suspect

him of wanting to seize the throne, and so he
kept out of his way.   How little he knew of
David's kindness, and his love for his father!
He was very like a great many people now
who are afraid of the Lord Jesus, because they
do not know how full of love His heart is.

Some years ago a British ship was cruising
off the coast of Africa trying to catch slave
dhows, the vessels in which the cruel slave-
traders carried away their captives.   They used
to attack the unprotected villages in Africa, and
after killing a great many of the poor, black
people, would carry away the rest, chiefly the
boys and the girls of the village, and sell them
as slaves.

One day the British ship caught sight of a
slaver, and gave chase, but it was some time
before they caught it.   When our sailors
boarded it they found it was filled with little
black boys and girls, crowded together in the
dark hold, many of them in a dreadful condition.
The poor children were terrified when they
saw the sailors, and it took some time to make
them understand that they were going to be
kind to them and to set them free.

The kind-hearted British tars found out
afterwards that the slavers had made them eager

to escape from their pursuers. The slave-traders pointed to the smoke coming from the funnels of the cruiser, and told the children that the Englishmen were getting ready their great big saucepans, as they meant to cook and eat them when they were caught ; and so the children were very frightened instead of welcoming their kind deliverers.

This is how Satan tries to deceive us and to make us want to get away from the Lord Jesus, who is seeking to deliver us and make us happy. We are afraid of Him because we do not know Him.

The place where Mephibosheth lived was called Lodebar, and like so many of the names in the Bible it had a meaning which is very appropriate. Lodebar means the place of " no pasture," and those who try to keep away from the Lord Jesus, because they are afraid of Him, always live in a place of no pasture. They are like the prodigal in the far country, who, when his money came to an end, " began to be in want " ; and was glad to eat even " the husks that the swine did eat, and no man gave to him "—he, too, lived in the place of no pasture.

But David was not satisfied to have Mephi-bosheth so far away from him, and he sent to fetch him from Lodebar.   Mephibosheth had no idea what David wanted, and probably was very much afraid at the summons.   When he heard David's voice speaking to him so kindly, he was greatly surprised.

David had not sent for him that he might put him in prison, but had called him to the palace to tell him that there was a place ready for him and that he would always find a welcome there.   Mephibosheth thought of his lameness, and felt that he was not fit to sit down at the king's table, but David did not mind this, and would not take any refusal.

Besides giving him a place at the royal table David restored to him the property that had belonged to his father Jonathan, and told Ziba, an old servant of his grandfather Saul, that in future he and his sons were to serve Mephibosheth.

How glad Mephibosheth must have been to exchange Lodebar, the place of no pasture, for the king's own palace and a seat at the king's own table!

This picture story is only a faint type of how the Lord Jesus treats those for whom He has done so much, and whom He has loved so dearly.   He does not merely send to fetch

them as David sent. The Lord Jesus came
Himself to the place of no pasture "to seek
and to save that which was lost," and now He
bids us welcome to His home.

David told Mephibosheth that he might
sit at his table "as one of the king's sons," but
those who come to the Lord Jesus are not
merely LIKE king's sons, they actually BECOME
God's children.   "Behold what manner of
love the Father hath bestowed upon us that we
should be called the sons of God: and such we
are." "As many as received Him, to them
gave He power to become the sons of God,
even to them that believe on His name." [1]

There is a great difference between David's
experience in Psalm xxiii. and that of Mephibosheth at Lodebar—between the green pastures
and the place of no pasture ; but when Mephibosheth had been brought into the presence of
the king, he could use the language of the
shepherd Psalm literally. He could say : "I
shall not want" ; he had reached the green
pastures and the king's house.

[1] We have another picture of Mephibosheth later which
gives us a glimpse of how dearly he loved David.   See p. 187.

TITLES OF JEHOVAH IN PSALM XXIII

JEHOVAH-ROHI [1] my Shepherd lives,
JEHOVAH-JIREH [2] my portion gives,
And such the wealth of His boundless store,
JEHOVAH-JOSEPH [3] adds more and more.
I cannot want mid the pastures green,
But follow on where my Lord has been.
JEHOVAH-SHALOM [4] with peace doth crown,
By quiet waters I lay me down ;
JEHOVAH-ROPKA [5] restores my soul,
His rod and staff will protect, control ;
JEHOVAH-TSIDKENU [6] leads the way,
Mid paths of righteousness day by day ;
Through death's dark valley I will not fear,
JEHOVAH-SHAMMAH [7] the Lord is there !
JEHOVAH-NISSI [8] waves overhead,
And midst my foes is a table spread ;
JEHOVAH-MEKADISHKEM [9] with oil my head anoints,
My cup o'erflows with blessing, which He in love
     appoints ;
His goodness and His mercy pursue me on my way,
And in JEHOVAH's mansion, I soon shall dwell for aye.
To-day as yesterday still the same,
JEHOVAH-JESUS is now His Name,
The same JEHOVAH of olden days,
For ever centre of endless praise.

[1] Ps. xxiii. 1.   [2] Gen. xxii. 14.   [3] Ps. cxv. 14.
[4] Judg. vi. 24.   [5] Ex. xv. 26.   [6] Jer. xxiii. 6.
[7] Ezek. xlviii. 35.   [8] Ex. xvii. 15.   [9] Ex. xxxi. 13 ; Lev. xx. 8.

DAVID ON THE
MOUNT OF OLIVES

"The King went forth, and all the people after him, and tarried in a place that was far off . . .

David went up by the ascent of Mount Olivet, and wept as he went up."

2 Samuel 15:17,30a

18

DAVID ON THE
MOUNT OF OLIVES

THE Old Testament types always fall far short of the great Antitype, for the men who foreshadowed the Lord Jesus in some points of their history, were sinful men, and so were great contrasts to Him. Thus it was with David. He fell into grievous sin, but yet God could say that he was a man after His own heart, for when he had sinned, he confessed it and was forgiven. But this sin brought sorrow into the palace, till at last David's own son Absalom committed a terrible crime, for he murdered his brother, and was obliged to fly from Jerusalem. Three times we read the words : " Absalom fled," " Absalom fled," " Absalom fled " ; and though David's heart longed after him he knew that it was not right to pass over such sin. But " David mourned for his son every day . . . and the soul of David longed to go forth unto Absalom."

At last some of his courtiers determined to persuade him to recall Absalom, and Joab, David's prime minister or commander-in-chief, sent for a wise woman to appeal to David. The petition which she pretended to make on her own behalf was really a plea for the recall of Absalom, and some of her words were very beautiful when we apply them to the Gospel, for she said of God : "Yet doth He devise means that His banished be not expelled from Him" (2 Sam. xiv. 14).

David was longing for an excuse to bring back his son, so he was easily persuaded to allow him to return ; and though for a time he would not see him, gradually Absalom was able to resume his place. But though these words are very beautiful when applied to God's wonderful plan of salvation, there is a very great contrast between God's way and David's. It is true that through the death of the Lord Jesus on the cross, God has devised means that banished sinners be not expelled from Him, but this is because sin has been judged and the punishment borne by our Saviour. God's plan involved the death of our Substitute, for the banished ones could only be brought back on the ground of perfect righteousness and justice.

It was not so with David. Absalom's sin was unjudged and unpunished. He was allowed to return, but his return brought no happiness to David.

Instead of honouring his father, he soon began to conspire against him, and to stir up a rebellion. He was a very handsome prince, and he won the hearts of the people by flatteries, persuading them that if only he were on the throne he would do much better for them than David. The mischief spread and "the conspiracy was strong ; for the people increased continually with Absalom," so that soon he gained his desire and they proclaimed him king. They acted as their descendants did long afterwards when they "denied the Holy One and the Just, and desired a murderer to be granted unto them" (Acts iii. 14).

David was obliged to leave his city and go forth as a fugitive with a little band of faithful followers. And at this point of his history we see in him again a type of the Lord Jesus, rejected by His nation, and weeping over Jerusalem. As we read of that sorrowful little procession climbing up the slopes of Olivet (2 Sam. xv. and xvi.), we are reminded of several scenes in the Lord's own history when

He too walked with His disciples on the same mount.

One word in Samuel links together David and David's greater Son, for we read that there David "was wont to worship God"; while in Luke we read that on that night in which the Lord was betrayed "He went, as He was wont, to the Mount of Olives" (2 Sam. xv. 32, R.V., *marg.*; Luke xxii. 39, 40). It was the familiar resort of both when they would pour out their heart to God.

The Mount of Olives will always be a specially hallowed place, for it was the last on which the Lord's feet stood when, leading His disciples over its brow "as far as to Bethany," "He was taken up, and a cloud received Him out of their sight." But this is not all: it will be the very next spot on earth's soil where those once pierced feet will stand, for the two men in white apparel who appeared to His disciples after His ascension said: "This same Jesus, which is taken up from you into heaven, shall so come in like manner as ye have seen Him go into heaven"; and we read in Zechariah xiv., "His feet shall stand in that day upon the Mount of Olives."

When David left his city we read "the

king went forth, and all the people after him, and tarried in a place that was far off." This is what the great Son of David has done. His own people, Israel, have said : " We will not have this man to reign over us " ; and He too has had to leave His city, and He is now " as a man taking a far journey " (Mark xiii. 34). But He has not left His city for ever, He intends to return, and so, like David, He is only tarrying in the place that is far off. Very soon " He that shall come will come, and will not tarry."

In 2 Sam. xv. 23 we read : " The king also himself passed over the brook Kidron " ; and in John xviii. 1 we are told that the Lord Jesus " went forth with His disciples over the brook Kidron, where was a garden, into the which He entered, and His disciples." " Kidron " means " blackness," and truly the King of Israel went down into blackness on that night before His crucifixion.

We are told that " David went up by the ascent of Olivet, and wept as he went up," and the people with him followed his example ; and here we have a foreshadowing of our Lord, who on the very same road wept over His rejection by Jerusalem. He was not leaving Jerusalem,

but was going into the city ; and in Luke xix.
37 we read : " When He was come nigh, even
now at the descent of the Mount of Olives, the
whole multitude of the disciples began to rejoice
and praise God with a loud voice " ; but
"When He was come near, He beheld the city,
and wept over it " (*v.* 41).

While His disciples were rejoicing, His
heart was full of sorrow.   The multitudes were
shouting " Hosanna ! " but He knew that in a
few days they would be crying, " Crucify Him !
crucify Him ! "   The sorrow of our Lord was
borne alone, for none understood His grief.
The sorrow of David was shared by his
servants, as they thought of the treatment he
had received.

They shared his danger also, for when
Shimei "went along on the hill's side over
against him, and cursed as he went, and threw
stones at him, and cast dust," he " cast stones at
David, and at all the servants of king David."
We can imagine how they would try and shield
their lord, and we know that they did not desert
him.   How different from the treatment which
the Lord received when " they all forsook Him
and fled " !

Shimei cast stones " at all the servants of

king David" because they were his servants ;
and if we are true followers of the Lord Jesus
we too shall have to share in His reproach.
He said to His disciples : " If the world hate
you, ye know that it hated Me before it hated
you." If we are walking close to Him we are
sure to come in for some of the stones, or at
least the dust. We may be certain that when
the kingdom was restored to David, he took
special delight in honouring those who had been
hit by the stones which were aimed at himself.
To us who share in our Lord's rejection now it
is promised that " if we suffer, we shall also
reign with Him " (see p. 188).

The little scene between David and Ittai is
very beautiful. He did not belong to the people
of Israel, and the king said to him : " Wherefore
goest thou also with us ? return to thy place . . .
for thou art a stranger, and also an exile. Where-
as thou camest but yesterday, should I this day
make thee go up and down with us ? " But
Ittai does not hesitate : it is true he has but just
come to know David, but that is enough : " As
the Lord liveth, and as my lord the king liveth,
surely in what place my lord the king shall be,
whether in death or life, even there also will
thy servant be." This is the language of every

heart which has been taught by the Holy Spirit to "say that Jesus is the Lord." If they have enlisted "but yesterday," they will prefer to take their place with the King in exile, rather than join the ranks of the usurper.

The true followers of David would not willingly remain in Jerusalem, for they could not have had any fellowship with Absalom's festivities; their place was outside the city. Are not many of God's children trying to be in both places at once, friendly with Absalom's followers, and yet professing to be on David's side? On which side are you?

BRINGING BACK
THE KING

"Now therefore why speak ye not a word
of bringing the king back?"

2 Samuel 19:10b

19

BRINGING BACK THE KING

THE insurrection was over, for Absalom was slain, but still David the king tarried in the " place that was far off." Israel had fled every man to his tent. How ashamed they must have felt of their behaviour, as they remembered their ingratitude to their king ! They saw their conduct at last in its true light, and we read that " all the people were at strife throughout all the tribes of Israel, saying, The king saved us out of the hand of our enemies, and he delivered us out of the hand of the Philistines ; and now he is fled out of the land for Absalom. And Absalom whom we anointed over us, is dead in battle " (2 Sam. xix. 9, 10).

What a sad confession ! They had to own that they had chosen a murderer, and rejected their king.

Here we have a faint picture of the coming

day when God "will pour upon the house of David, and upon the inhabitants of Jerusalem, the spirit of grace and of supplications ; and they shall look upon Me whom they have pierced, and they shall mourn for him as one mourneth for his only son, and shall be in bitterness for him, as one that is in bitterness for his first-born " (Zech. xii. 10).

Of that day God says : " There shall ye remember your ways, and all your doings . . . and ye shall loathe yourselves in your own sight " (Ezek. xx. 43).

They will be ashamed also to think how they too have been deceived by the one who has " come in his own name," and him they have received (John v. 43). But most of all they will mourn because of their treatment of their King, and in that day they will with shame confess : " He was despised and we esteemed Him not " (Is. liii. 3).

As the men of Israel reminded themselves of the great deliverance which David had wrought when he slew their enemy Goliath, so the children of Israel will understand at last that the Lord Jesus accomplished for them a far greater deliverance ; and they will say : " He was wounded for our transgressions, He

was bruised for our iniquities ; the chastisement
of our peace was upon Him, and with His
stripes we are healed " (Is. liii. 5).

But before that day of Israel's awakening
the Lord Jesus is coming back again to receive
to Himself His Church, all His own people
who have been saved during the time of His
absence and of Israel's rejection. Then "the
Lord Himself shall descend from heaven with
a shout, with the voice of the archangel and
with the trump of God : and the dead in
Christ shall rise first. Then we which are
alive and remain shall be caught up together
with them in the clouds, to meet the Lord
in the air " (1 Thess. iv. 16, 17).

Almost His last words to His disciples
before He died were a promise of His return :
" I will come again and receive you unto
Myself ; " and the closing words of the Book
of the Revelation, and of the whole Bible, are
His last message on this subject : " Surely I
come quickly." He really meant what He
said, and many of His people believe that His
coming must be very near at hand.

After Absalom had been slain there seemed
nothing to prevent the king from returning.
But there was just one thing. He was evidently

waiting to be brought back by the men of his tribe, the men of Judah.   Others in Israel were indignant to think that those who were most nearly related to him had not insisted on his return.   " Now, therefore, why speak ye not a word of bringing the king back ? "   Then David himself sent a message by the faithful priests, Zadok and Abiathar, saying : " Speak unto the elders of Judah, saying, Why are ye the last to bring the king back to his house ? . . . Ye are my brethren, ye are my bones and my flesh ; wherefore then are ye the last to bring back the king ? "   And the message took instant effect.   " He bowed the heart of all the men of Judah, even as the heart of one man ; so that they sent this word unto the king, Return thou " (2 Sam. xix. 11–15).

It was the message of the king himself that wrought the change : " Where the word of a king is there is power " (Eccles. viii. 4), and that made the people say with one accord : " Return thou."   " So the king returned."

Let us, then, who do believe that He is coming back again, and who are longing for His return, pray that He may bow hearts thus, so that multitudes of His people may gladden

His heart and "speak a word of bringing the king back."

Immediately after this Mephibosheth had a memorable audience with the king. David did not understand why he had not gone forth with him, but Mephibosheth explained that his lameness and Ziba's treachery had prevented him. He had sorely mourned the absence of David "from the day the king departed until the day he came again in peace"; but Ziba had so thoroughly misrepresented his master to David that David had taken away Mephibosheth's property, and had given it to Ziba.

But though Ziba had robbed him, Mephibosheth was happy, and said : "Yea, let him take all, forasmuch as my lord the king is come again in peace unto his own house" (2 Sam. xix. 24–30). That was the great thing, nothing else mattered. Ziba might say what he liked, he might slander and rob him of his property ; the king had come back again, and Mephibosheth was glad !

This is a beautiful little picture of how those who love the Lord should feel concerning His absence. If our heart is right with Him, we feel we cannot be really happy while He is

absent.   The festivities in Jerusalem in honour
of the usurper had no attraction for Mephibosheth's loyal heart.   He was mourning while
others rejoiced.   If we have tasted of the love
of the Lord Jesus, we feel that the world and
its pleasures cannot satisfy our hearts ; and
when He comes how small and insignificant
everything else will seem !

After our Lord Jesus Christ has received us
to Himself at His coming again "we must all
appear before the judgment-seat of Christ."
But He will not make mistakes as David did.
No one will be misjudged by Him.   " Every
man's work shall be made manifest: for the
day shall declare it, because it shall be revealed
by fire ; and the fire shall try every man's work
of what sort it is " (1 Cor. iii. 13).

And then the rewards will be distributed,
and the deeds of devotion will meet with His
word of commendation, His " Well done, good
and faithful servant, . . . enter thou into the
joy of thy Lord."

David thought first of those who had
ministered to him and who had shared his
sufferings.   Barzillai, the Gileadite, had done
much for David and his followers when they
were "hungry and weary and thirsty in the

wilderness " as they fled with him from Absalom
(2 Sam. xvii. 27–29).   He had brought an
abundant supply of provisions, and even of
luxuries, for their need, and this was not
forgotten by David.   When he was once more
returning to Jerusalem, Barzillai came forth to
welcome him, and the king wanted to reward
him for all that he had done.   He offered him
a place with him in his palace.   " Why should
the king recompense it me with such a reward ? "
To be with our Lord, near to Him in His
glory, will be the Lord's " recompence of reward " for loyalty to Himself and to His service.

Though Barzillai himself was not able to
accompany David to Jerusalem, for he was an
old man and did not wish to be a burden to the
king, he asked that the reward might be trans-
ferred to his son Chimham, so Chimham went
on with the king.   David evidently gave him
some of his own private property in Bethlehem
(Jer. xli. 17), and it is said that Chimham's
house afterwards became the inn at Bethlehem,
in the stable of which the Lord Jesus was born.

David never forgot those who had shared
his sorrows, and in his dying charge to Solomon
his son, he said : " Shew kindness unto the sons
of Barzillai the Gileadite, and let them be of

those that eat at thy table : for so they came to me when I fled because of Absalom thy brother" (1 Kings ii. 7). This reminds us of the words of our Lord to His disciples just before He went to the cross : "Ye are they which have continued with Me in My temptations. And I appoint unto you a kingdom, as My Father hath appointed unto Me ; that ye may eat and drink at My table in My kingdom " (Luke xxii. 28–30). This was said to the apostles, but it is also true that "if we suffer we shall also reign with Him."

BUILDING THE TEMPLE

"The house that is to be builded for the Lord must be exceeding magnifical, of fame and of glory throughout all countries."

1 Chronicles 22:5b

20

BUILDING THE TEMPLE

DAVID had set his heart on building a house for God. He looked at his own beautiful palace, and compared it with the Tabernacle that had been made so long ago in the wilderness. " See now," he said, "I dwell in a house of cedar, but the ark of God dwelleth within curtains" (2 Sam. vii. 2).

But though God was pleased with David for wishing to do it, He would not allow him to accomplish his purpose. David had fought many battles, and had often shed blood. The Temple of God must be built by his son Solomon (peaceable), the "man of rest" (1 Chron. xxii. 9)—a type of the Prince of Peace. The name chosen for him by God was Jedidiah, which means "Beloved of the Lord" (2 Sam. xii. 25).

But though David might not build the

Temple he at once began to make preparation.
"The house that is to be builded for the Lord
must be exceeding magnifical, of fame and of
glory throughout all countries," he said. "I
will therefore now make preparation for it"
(1 Chron. xxii. 5).

This chapter tells us of the vast store of
material and of gold and silver that he set aside,
as he said in his "poverty." What preparation
the Lord Jesus made for the Temple that was to
be built for God, and at what a cost!

Before his death David had already fixed
on the site, and had purchased it. There had
been a time of great sorrow in Israel, for God
had sent a terrible plague upon the people, as
a punishment for David's sin. He had become
proud of his high position and power, and in
order to feed his pride he had decided to
number the people; but there seems to have
been no recognition of the law that whenever
the people were numbered, half a shekel was
to be paid for each one, as redemption money,
and so the judgment fell.

David was given by God the choice of three
evils—seven years of famine, three years of
flight before the enemy, or three days' pestilence.
David said to the prophet who had been sent

to him : " I am in a great strait " ; but he decided that he would rather fall into the hand of God than into the hand of man, and he chose the pestilence.   It was a terrible time, for many died ; but when the angel of destruction stretched out his hand upon Jerusalem to destroy it, the Lord repented Him of the evil, and said to the angel : " It is enough, stay now thine hand."

David himself saw the angel, he saw the uplifted sword, and he besought God to have mercy on his people.   The sin was his, not theirs.   And when he pleaded, the answer came, telling him to build an altar and offer a sacrifice. God's judgment can only be averted by the shedding of blood.

David had seen the angel of the Lord with the drawn sword in his hand standing between earth and heaven, just over the threshing-floor of Ornan, or Araunah, the Jebusite, and God told David that this was the place for the altar —and this was the place also where the Temple was to be built.   We read in 2 Chron. iii. 1 that it was in Mount Moriah, the very spot where the wonderful scene of Gen. xxii. had taken place.   There the father had not spared his son (see pp. 21, 22) ; there Abraham sheathed his knife because a substitute was found ; and as David saw the fire fall from heaven upon the altar, in token that God had accepted his sacrifice, he " saw that the Lord had answered him," for the angel " put up his sword again into the sheath thereof " (1 Chron. xxi. 27, 28).

What more appropriate place could be found for the Temple of Jehovah ? David had already bought the threshing-floor and the oxen for fifty shekels of silver (2 Sam. xxiv. 24), but when he saw the sheathed sword he cried : " This is the house of the Lord God, and this is the altar of the burnt-offering for Israel " ; and so he bought the whole place, the whole rock on which the Temple was afterwards built, for six hundred shekels of gold (1 Chron. xxi. 25 ; xxii. 1, 2). And now he could begin to prepare the stones for the Temple. " He set masons to hew wrought stones to build the house of God."

We know from the New Testament what these stones typified, for we read : " Ye also as living stones are built up a spiritual house " (1 Peter ii. 5) ; " Jesus Christ Himself being the chief corner stone ; in whom all the building fitly framed together, groweth unto an holy temple in the Lord " (Eph. ii. 20, 21).

When Solomon came to the throne he soon

began to build the house of the Lord. "The house when it was in building, was built of stone made ready before it was brought thither : so that there was neither hammer, nor axe, nor any tool of iron, heard in the house while it was in building" (1 Kings vi. 7). All the preparation was done beneath the Temple area. Wonderful quarries have been found in underground Jerusalem where the stones were prepared, there they were shaped and chiselled.

In the Book of Proverbs, Solomon says : "Prepare thy work without, and make it fit for thyself in the field ; and afterwards build thine house" (Prov. xxiv. 27). This is what Solomon did, and what God is doing. "The field is the world," and here God is making the stones "fit for Himself" ; and when they are all ready the house will be completed. There will be no chiselling done in heaven, no heavy hammer's blow heard or felt there.

While the Tabernacle may be taken to typify Christ and His people in wilderness days, the Temple points rather to Christ and His Church in the glory. The Tabernacle stood upon desert sands, the Temple had a floor of gold. The Tabernacle had no outward beauty, it was covered with skins, unattractive to the eye, insignificant in size.   The Temple was exceeding magnifical, of noble proportions, covered with gold gleaming in the sunlight. God's house was no longer of humble exterior, but was glorious to behold—"the palace not for man, but for the Lord God" (1 Chron. xxix. 1).   And so will it be with the people of God by and by, when in resurrection beauty they will reflect His glory.

Solomon prepared many beautiful vessels for use in the Temple, and these teach us the same lessons as the stones.   "In the plain of Jordan did the king cast them, in the clay ground."

"The vessels of mercy which God had afore prepared unto glory" (Rom. ix. 23) will all have been moulded in the clay ground of earth, in the valley of the river of death (Jordan).

The story of the dedication of the Temple, when the work was finished and all the beautiful vessels were brought into their place, is a wonderful picture of the scene in the glory when all the people of God are gathered Home at last.   We may compare Rev. v. with 2 Chron. v.

Until the Temple was built in Jerusalem,

there had been a divided choir in Israel. Some of the singers had their place in the Tabernacle which was set up in Gibeon, others ministered before the Ark in the tent which David had made for it in Jerusalem ; but now the two choirs are united, and we read that " the singers . . . all of them . . . being arrayed in white linen . . . stood at the east end of the altar," where the ashes of the sacrifices were poured out—the place of accepted sacrifice. And then the harps were sounded and the song arose triumphantly. " The singers were as one to make one sound to be heard in praising and thanking the Lord . . . saying, For He is good ; for His mercy endureth for ever " (2 Chron. v. 12, 13).

No voices were silent, there were no discords, but all was perfect harmony in that trained choir. It is only a faint picture of that far more glorious scene when those who have been feebly trying to praise God on earth are united to those who praise Him perfectly in heaven. " And they sang a new song, saying, Thou art worthy " (Rev. v. 9). They too will be arrayed in white raiment, " having every one of them harps," and " on their heads crowns of gold," as they " give glory and honour and

thanks to Him that sitteth on the throne"
(Rev. iv. 4, 9).

Ear never heard such music as then will
rise from the lips of the redeemed. As we
look at this wonderful picture of the building
of Solomon's Temple, we may ask ourselves
three questions : Am I a stone that is being
prepared for God's Temple ? Am I a precious
vessel which He is moulding and preparing
for glory ? Am I being trained to take my
place in the heavenly choir ? How would you
answer these questions ? Can you answer "Yes"
to all three ?

THE QUEEN
OF SHEBA

"She said to the king, It was a true report that I heard in mine own land... Howbeit I believed not the words, until I came, and mine eyes had seen it: and, behold, the half was not told me."

1 Kings 10:6,7a

21

THE QUEEN OF SHEBA

THE news of Solomon's glory and wisdom travelled far and wide among the neighbouring countries. In those days every road led to Jerusalem. Merchandise of all descriptions was brought to the wealthy city, and the merchant caravans, as they returned to their distant homes, carried with them strange tidings of the splendours of Solomon's court. The news even penetrated into Central Africa, borne thither, it may be, by some of the returning traders who had been to Jerusalem with tusks from the land of elephants for Solomon's "ivory palaces."

The Queen of Sheba—a country to the south of Egypt and Ethiopia [1]—was greatly

---

[1] It has been stated by some that Sheba was in Arabia ; but from the Lord's words—" the uttermost parts of the earth," and from the description of the journey and of the presents brought to Solomon, it seems much more probable that it was beyond Ethiopia and Abyssinia. There are many traditions also to this effect.

interested in the rumours concerning the great king, and the still greater God whom he worshipped. She only half believed their truth, but made up her mind that she would go and see for herself. So she summoned her black ministers of state and her servants, collected a great quantity of gold, spices, and precious stones as a present for the great king, and started on her journey across the desert, with a long cavalcade of camels—"a very great train."

Jerusalem at this time was always filled with strangers, but such a company of coloured people must have made a considerable stir, and Solomon soon heard of the arrival of the black queen and her suite.

At the dedication of the Temple, God had put it into his heart to pray for just such a case : "Concerning a stranger that is not of Thy people Israel, but cometh out of a far country for Thy name's sake" (1 Kings viii. 41). This was just what the Queen of Sheba had done, for it was "when she heard of the fame of Solomon concerning the name of the Lord that she came to prove him" (1 Kings x. 1). Solomon prayed if such a stranger should "come and pray toward this house, hear Thou in heaven Thy dwelling-place, and do according to all that the

stranger calleth to Thee for." This then was
an opportunity for Solomon to act in the spirit
of his prayer, and to help towards the answer.

The Queen of Sheba was amazed at all that
she saw. She had thought her own little court
was splendid, but it was nothing to this. She
had expected that the glowing reports must be
exaggerated, but now she acknowledged that it
was just the opposite. " The half was not told
me." She was specially struck with the gor-
geously apparelled officials that waited on the
king, his vast retinue of courtiers, and the cupbearers that stood behind him when he feasted.

And then the wonderful wisdom of Solomon !
Words failed her when she tried to express her
admiration. She had been perplexed with so
many difficulties before she came, but he
answered all her questions, even anticipating
them, so that he explained just what she wanted
to know before she even asked the question.
We read : " When she was come to Solomon
she communed with him of all that was in her
heart, and Solomon told her all her questions ;
there was not anything hid from the king that
he told her not." Is there any wonder that
she said to the king : " It was a true report
that I heard in mine own land of thy acts and

of thy wisdom.   Howbeit I believed not the
words, until I came, and mine eyes had seen
it ; and, behold, the half was not told me ; thy
wisdom and prosperity exceedeth the fame
which I heard " ? (1 Kings x. 6, 7).

There can be no doubt that this scene was
typical of the way in which a sinner comes to
the Lord Jesus, for He claimed Solomon as a
type of Himself. " The queen of the South
shall rise up in the judgment with this genera-
tion, and shall condemn it : for she came from
the uttermost parts of the earth to hear the
wisdom of Solomon ; and, behold, a greater than
Solomon is here " (Matt. xii. 42).

How abundantly she was rewarded for her
long journey ! She had but heard a few
rumours from those who had themselves seen
" Solomon in all his glory," but though she
only half believed the reports, they were enough
to make her long to see for herself, and so she
acted upon them.

How many, in the favoured days in which
we are living, have heard all their lives about
the " Greater than Solomon," but have never
acted on what they know, have never come
themselves to find out if He is really as good
and as gracious, as wise and as wealthy, as men

say ! The Queen of Sheba puts such to shame. She owned when she had really seen the glory of the king that she had never believed it before. "I believed not until I came, and mine eyes had seen." Her personal experience soon satisfied her as to the truth of what she had heard ; and so it is with those who come to the Lord Jesus. They may have heard about Him for years, but it is only when they themselves come that they really believe.

The story reminds us of the testimony of the men of Sychar. The woman at the well had met her Saviour. She drank of the water that He alone could give, and straightway there bubbled up a well in her own heart. She left her water-pot when she got the well, and hurried to the men of the city with the astonishing news : "Come, see a Man, which told me all things that ever I did" (John iv. 29). Her testimony was enough to make them come, but it was seeing Him and hearing Him that won their hearts ; and they said : "Now we believe, not because of thy saying ; for we have heard Him ourselves and know that this is indeed the Saviour of the world" (v. 42). Such personal knowledge never comes from hearsay.

How wonderfully Solomon answered all the Queen of Sheba's questions, and " a greater than Solomon is here " !   He can meet all our difficulties, for He knows our very thoughts. Many a one, on coming to Christ, has found that the difficulties they had before they came have vanished directly they have heard His voice ; and He is always ready to commune with us of all that is in our hearts.

Amongst the many things that attracted the Queen of Sheba was the standing of Solomon's servants, their apparel, and his cupbearers.   All this added to the majesty and splendour of his court.   The servants of the Lord Jesus can do much to bring honour to their Master by their attitude, the promptness with which they run His errands, their devotion to His person, and their apparel when they show that they have indeed " put on the Lord Jesus Christ " (Rom. xii. 14).

And the king's cupbearers—how often have they won souls to Him !   A " cup of cold water " given in His Name has often been the means of winning a heart, and it will in no wise lose its reward.

Another thing that delighted the Queen of Sheba was the meat of his table.   She never

had tasted such food in all her life.   But most
wonderful of all, she was allowed to see " his
burnt-offering which he offered in the House
of the Lord " (1 Kings x. 5, R.V.), and " there
was no more spirit in her."

It is when we see Christ Jesus our Lord as the
great burnt-offering, the sweet-savour offering,
that our hearts are bowed in adoration, as we
learn for the first time that we can be " accepted
in the Beloved," for this is the teaching of the
burnt-offering.   The queen did not belong to
Israel, and she could not feel that that burnt-
offering was offered for her.   She could only look
on and wonder, but we may lay our hand on the
offering (see p. 109) and say : " It is for me."

Everyone who thus comes to the Lord Jesus
will exclaim with the Queen of Sheba : " The
half was not told me."   In other words, as we
read in Job : " The secrets of wisdom . . . are
double to that which is " (Job xi. 6).   We
never can tell to others anything approaching
to half or even a quarter of His worthiness.

The story ends by telling us that the queen
" turned and went to her own country," and
though none of those who come to the
" Greater than Solomon " are ever sent back
to the far country, He does say : " Go home

to thy friends, and tell." Before leaving she presented to the king the treasures she had brought—the gold, the precious stones, the sweet smelling spices, "a very great store."

The king valued her presents very highly, and never forgot them. He commemorated them in the Psalm in which he speaks prophetically of the coming King to whom "the kings of Sheba shall offer gifts": "To Him shall be given of the gold of Sheba" (Ps. lxxii. 10, 15). Her gifts were emblems of all those which will be offered to "the King in His beauty" when He comes to reign.

As for the spices, we read "there came no such abundance" (1 Kings x. 10); and the Chronicles account adds, "neither was there any such spice" (2 Chron. ix. 9). We, too, can offer to the King precious spices when we give to Him the love of our hearts. "How fair is thy love, my sister, my spouse! how much better is thy love than wine! and the smell of thine ointments than all spices!" (Song of Sol. iv. 10).

What she gave was nothing to what she received. "King Solomon gave unto the Queen of Sheba all her desire; whatsoever she asked, beside that which Solomon gave her of his royal bounty " (1 Kings x. 13). It must be in proportion to his wealth, "according to the hand of King Solomon " (*marg.*). We have all the unsearchable riches of Christ to draw upon, and when He gives, He does so "exceeding abundantly above all that we ask or think."

It may be that in the story of the Ethiopian eunuch (Acts viii.) there is a faint echo of the Queen of Sheba's visit to Solomon. We can imagine that when she returned to her own land she carried with her some knowledge of the God of Israel, and the truth may have spread to the surrounding lands, so that God had worshippers even in Central Africa. More than a thousand years afterwards we read of an official from the court of the Queen of the Ethiopians, who had come to Jerusalem in order that he might worship Jehovah in the place where He had set His Name. The eunuch was returning home without having heard of the Saviour who had come to save sinners ; but God knew all about him, and prepared a way by which he should meet with one who could teach him. All heaven was interested in the salvation of this single soul.

Philip, who had been having a time of great blessing in Samaria, was commanded by the

Angel of the Lord to leave the happy work, and take a road through the desert country round Gaza. It seemed a strange command for a busy worker to be told to leave the crowds where he was so much needed, but God wanted to bring him into contact with the African officer who was all ready to receive the Good News. Philip obeyed the call without knowing why he was being sent in this direction, but when he saw the chariot, the Spirit of God at once told him to speak to the black man. How eagerly he ran forward! He noticed that the Ethiopian was reading aloud from the prophet Isaiah, perhaps from a roll just purchased in Jerusalem. It was not by chance that he happened to be studying that wonderful 53rd chapter. What a delightful task for Philip to tell him, as he had told Nathaniel: "We have found Him, of whom Moses in the law, and the prophets, did write" (John i. 45)! Beginning "at the same Scripture, he preached unto him Jesus." The Ethiopian eunuch received the Gospel at once and was baptized by the roadside, confessing: "I believe that Jesus Christ is the Son of God." As he went on his way rejoicing we may be sure that he too could say: "The half was not told me."

NAAMAN THE SYRIAN

"Many lepers were in Israel in the time of Eliseus the prophet; and none of them was cleansed, saving Naaman the Syrian."

Luke 4:27

22

NAAMAN THE SYRIAN

THE commander-in-chief of the Syrian army was a great man. He was very brave and had often been victorious in battle, especially on one occasion when "by him the Lord had given deliverance to Syria." His king thought a great deal of him, and he was a universal favourite, for many a time he had returned from the war in triumph, the hero of all the people. But suddenly all his brilliant career was shadowed by a terrible disaster.

One day he noticed a white spot somewhere on his skin. He was startled, for it looked so much like that dreaded disease, leprosy. He watched it for a few days, and saw that it had spread, and though probably he managed to hide it for a short time it soon became known to every-one : "Naaman is a leper." If he had been an Israelite, he would have been obliged to leave his home at once, and go forth without the city, so that no one else might be defiled ; but though this was not the law in Syria, the disease was the same. It very soon put a stop to his public life, and it would finally have caused his death.

During one of his campaigns the Syrians had invaded the land of Israel, and among the captives they had carried away to Syria a little Israelitish maiden who was given by Naaman to his wife ; and when this little slave girl heard that Naaman was a leper she was greatly concerned. Though a slave, she was evidently very fond of her master, and did so wish that something could be done to cure him.

She thought of her own land and of the mighty prophet of whom she had often heard before she was taken captive. She remembered how he had worked many miracles, and had actually raised to life a little boy who had died suddenly from sunstroke ; and she felt sure that he would be able even to cure leprosy. So she said to her mistress : "I do wish my lord Naaman could go and see Elisha the prophet in Samaria, for he would recover him of his leprosy." Her mistress eagerly questioned her, and the words of the little slave girl were repeated by one and another till everyone knew what she had said. Naaman himself heard it, and one of the courtiers told the king.

The Syrians had never heard of such a thing as a man being cured of the dreadful disease, and it seemed too good to be true that Naaman could recover ; but though they scarcely believed it was possible, it was worth trying. Naaman was becoming much worse, the disease had made rapid progress, and already his flesh was being eaten away, so the king decided that he must go to the land of Israel at once. But instead of sending to the prophet himself, the king of Syria wrote a letter to the king of Israel, and Naaman started off, not this time at the head of an army, but with a few servants and a handsome present.

The king of Israel was dismayed when he read the letter and the startling message : " Behold, I have sent Naaman my servant to thee that thou mayest recover him of his leprosy." The son of Ahab and of the wicked Jezebel knew very little of the prophet's power, not nearly as much as the little slave girl ; but he did know that only the power of God could heal a leper, and he rent his clothes, exclaiming : " Am I God, to kill and to make alive ? " He felt sure that the king of Syria only wanted to pick a quarrel with him.

But Elisha heard that the Syrian commander-in-chief had arrived and that the king had rent his clothes, so he sent word to him : "Let him come now to me, and he shall know (though you have forgotten it) that there is a prophet in Israel."

Now Naaman was a very important personage in his own country, and he was accustomed to being treated with great respect, and with much ceremony. He did not mind driving in his chariot to the prophet's house, but he expected that the prophet would be very proud to have a visit from such a great man, and that he would come out to him, and, calling upon the name of the Lord his God, would make a number of passes over him, and then he would be cured.

But Naaman not only needed that his flesh should become like the flesh of a little child, but that his heart should become like the heart of a little child. God would not cure him till he was humble and obedient. When Elisha sent out a message to him, and told him to go and wash in Jordan seven times, promising that then the flesh that had been eaten away should come again, and he should be clean, Naaman was very angry, and rather than do such a thing was prepared to go home at once, in a rage. The very idea of asking him to go

and dip in that little river Jordan ! The rivers
Abana and Pharpar that ran through the city
of Damascus were far greater.

But he had some wise servants who succeeded in pacifying him. They said : " My
father, if the prophet had bid thee do some
great thing, wouldest thou not have done it ?
How much rather then, when he saith to thee,
Wash and be clean ? " Happily for himself,
and for us too, or we should never have had
the story, Naaman allowed himself to be persuaded, and he started once more.

It was quite a journey to the Jordan, nearly
five-and-twenty miles as the crow flies, and
much farther probably through the winding
valleys. A good many of the Israelites, it may
be, followed to see what would happen, and
eagerly they all watched as he descended from
his chariot and entered the river.

He dipped himself in the water, and looked
at his diseased flesh. No change, just the
same ! Again he dipped himself, and still
again, but each time there was no improvement.
Six times he came up just as bad as when he
had gone in first, but the seventh time, oh joy,
the leprosy was all gone ! There was not a
single trace of it left.

What a different journey back to Samaria ! How delighted they all felt ! The charioteer whipped up the horses, and as quickly as possible they stood before the prophet's house once more. Elisha came gladly to the door this time, and listened to Naaman's grateful thanks. " Behold, now I know that there is no God in all the earth, but in Israel." It was very natural that Naaman should want to give Elisha a handsome present ; but no, Elisha would not accept any payment from him.

The reason is very plain when we see that the whole scene is a wonderful type of sin, and its remedy. God's salvation is absolutely free. It is "without money and without price" ; and if Elisha had allowed Naaman to give him anything, he would have spoilt God's type. This is what Gehazi his servant did afterwards. He thought it was a great pity that something should not be made out of Naaman, so Naaman had no sooner got out of sight, than Gehazi ran after him, and, pretending to give a message from Elisha, asked for money and garments. Naaman gave him twice as much money as he had asked, and two changes of raiment ; but Gehazi had spoilt the type, and, because of this, the leprosy of Naaman came upon him.

Throughout Scripture leprosy is used as a type of sin, because of its corruption, its defilement, its contagion, and its fatal results. Naaman had all that his heart could wish, "*but* he was a leper": that spoilt everything. When he first went to Elisha, and was told that the remedy was such an easy thing, he said in his anger: "Behold I THOUGHT the prophet would have done something very different; I THOUGHT there would have been an important ceremony." But his thoughts were all wrong.

God says: "My thoughts are not your thoughts, neither are your ways My ways." Before we come to the Lord Jesus we think all sorts of wrong thoughts about His way of salvation; but when we have seen how He died on the cross to put away our sin, and have accepted Himself and His work, instead of saying: "I THOUGHT," we can say, as Naaman did: "Now I KNOW." Many people think it impossible to say: "I know I am saved; I know I am forgiven; I know I am healed." Naaman did not think it impossible. He had only to look at the place where the leprosy had been and he could be quite certain that he was cured; but he did not *feel* any better until he had done what the prophet had told him.

Like Naaman, many people think that
God's way is too easy. To look and live is
such a little thing ! but though it is easy for
us it was not easy for the Lord Jesus. He had
to lay down His life ; and we must be identified
with Him in His death too, as Naaman was in
symbol—for Jordan means death. God has
only one way of saving sinners. Rich and
poor, small and great, all are lepers, and all can
be healed in His appointed way.

What rejoicings there were in Damascus
when Naaman reached home ! His wife and
all the household were looking out for his
arrival. Some of them, it may be, were watching on the roof for the first sign of the chariots,
and how eagerly they greeted him ! They
hardly needed to ask : " Are you healed ? Did
the prophet cure you ? " His face and the
faces of all the company must have shown what
had happened, as they cried : " Perfectly whole,
clean every whit ! "

We may be sure that one of the first things
that Naaman did, after he had had an audience
with the king, was to send for the little slave girl
and thank her. How she must have rejoiced
to think that the few words she had spoken
had had such a result. There is no joy like

that of being able to lead a needy sinner to the
One who can heal his soul's disease. Even a
child can do this, by simply telling what he or
she knows about the Lord Jesus.

During the days of our Lord's Ministry
many lepers were cleansed. On one occasion
as He was passing through Samaria and Galilee,
and was about to enter into a certain village, ten
men that were lepers, who had been standing
" afar off " because of the terrible disease, called
loudly to Him : " Master, have mercy on us."
The Lord Jesus did not work an instantaneous
miracle, as they probably expected, and as
Naaman had thought Elisha would have done,
but He sent them to the priest.

A law had been given by Moses concerning
a healed leper (Lev. xiv.), but we have no record
that it had been carried out until this time. He
was to be examined by the priest, and if he pro-
nounced him clean, two little sparrows were to
be offered. One was to be slain, and the other,
after having been sprinkled with its blood, was
to be allowed to fly away. Certain rites were
to be performed, so that the man might be restored to his place amongst the people of God,
as though he had never been a leper.

Leprosy had shut him out from their camp

or from their dwellings.   He might not approach to the Temple.   Sin shuts us out from the presence of God, but when the sin has been put away, on the ground of the death and resurrection of the Lord Jesus—typified by the two birds—we are justified, and may have access to His presence as though we had never sinned.

As the ten lepers went to the priest the miracle took place.   They felt they were healed. They looked at each other and saw no mark of the fatal disease.   Nine of them hurried on eagerly to the priest, but one and only one, a despised Samaritan, felt he could not go a step farther.   He must return immediately to thank the One who had healed him.   " With a loud voice he glorified God, and fell down on his face, giving Him thanks."   Not merely was he the only one out of the ten who gave thanks, so that the Lord asked : " Where are the nine ? " but he was the only one in all the Gospels of whom it is recorded.   Was there no other occasion on which the Lord Jesus was thanked ? The silence concerning others who were healed is sadly suggestive.   As old Christopher Ness wrote so quaintly (A.D. 1678) : " God hath but the tenth of praises, and 'tis ten to one whether you preach out His praise."

LESSONS FOR
SONS OF THE PROPHETS

"That ye may know ... what is the exceeding greatness of His power to us-ward who believe, according to the working of His mighty power."

Ephesians 1:18,19

23

LESSONS FOR

SONS OF THE PROPHETS

1. THE LOST AXEHEAD

THE lives of the great prophets Elijah and Elisha made many young men in Israel wish to consecrate themselves to God, and the number of the sons of the prophets increased greatly. Many of the miracles of Elisha are connected with them, and the spiritual lessons we learn from these incidents are just the lessons that we need to-day in connection with service for the Lord.

On one occasion some of them came to Elisha to tell him that the house in which they dwelt together was too small. They must rebuild, for this earliest of theological colleges needed enlarging. If they moved to a new place, and built a new house, would Elisha approve, and would he go with them? To each question he gave his assent.

And so they went to the borders of the river Jordan where there was a wood, and began to cut down trees for the building; but while they were thus busily engaged, one of the young men met with an accident. The head of the axe which he was using suddenly flew off and fell into the river. It was out of sight in a moment at the bottom of the stream. What was he to do? for to make matters worse, as he told Elisha: "Alas, master, it was borrowed!"

It was very wise of him to go to the prophet, for he and he alone knew what to do. The man of God asked where it fell, and, being shown the place, he cut down a branch from an adjoining tree and cast it into the river; and, wonderful to relate, the iron at once floated and came ashore. Elisha told the young man to pick it up, and he had only to put out his hand and take it to himself. Here was a miracle indeed!

The iron was heavy, and had sunk to the bottom of the river. There it lay in the mire and the mud. It was helpless, it could do nothing to raise itself. Even if it could have struggled, it would only have got more mud upon it, and would have sunk deeper and deeper. While it lay there it was useless also. It was not fulfilling the purpose for which it was made. Is not this a striking picture of the helplessness of the sinner sunk in the mire and the clay of sin and death, unable to lift himself, and lying there useless and defiled ?

What hope is there for such ? None, but in the Branch, who typifies the Lord Jesus. He is called in Zech. iii. 8 : " My Servant, The BRANCH " ; and again in chapter vi. 12 : " Behold the Man whose Name is The BRANCH." There is no mistake as to who this is, for the prophet goes on to say that He is the One who " shall build the Temple of the Lord ; and He shall bear the glory, and shall sit and rule upon His throne, and He shall be a Priest upon His throne." He is the same One who can sweeten bitter waters (see p. 80).

The man who had lost the axe-head consulted with the man of God on the banks of the river. He wanted the axe-head so much. What could be done to recover it ? How wonderful was the consultation that took place between God the Father and God the Son over lost sinners ! They wanted to recover that which was lost. Only one thing would save the axe-head. The branch must be cut down and flung into the Jordan, the river of death (p. 222). The Lord Jesus must die. He must leave the light and glory of the Father's throne and descend to the place of death into which the sinner had fallen.

When it was cast into the river the branch at once began to exercise its miracle-working power on the iron in the mud. No one can explain how it was done, and no one can explain the drawing power of the Lord Jesus. The helpless iron felt the power of the branch, and helpless sinners feel the power of the Saviour and are lifted right up out of the mire of sin, till the One who has lost them puts out His hand and draws them to Himself, and is able to use them in His service.

The young man who had lost the axe-head did not say : "I cannot use it again, it has been right down in the mire of the river," and the Lord Jesus never says of any who have felt His attracting power, and have been raised out of the place of death, that He cannot use them because they have been defiled with sin. However deeply they have sunk, His power can lift them, and in His hand they can be useful to Him even in the work of building His house.

2. DEATH IN THE POT

Another of the sons of the prophets got into trouble. He made a mistake that might have brought serious evil to himself and to his companions. It was a time of dearth, and food was scarce, but when Elisha was with them his power prevented them from being in want.

One day they were sitting around him, listening perhaps to his teaching and his memories of Elijah. When the time came for them to have their meal, Elisha told his servant to set on the great pot and make a good soup for the sons of the prophets. One of them, anxious to help, ran out to gather herbs ; and, finding a plant with fruit upon it, gathered as many of the gourds or berries as he could carry, and poured them into the pot. He was quite unconscious that he had been gathering poison, but when his companions began to take their pottage they recognised the bitter flavour of the wild fruit, and exclaimed with dismay : "O thou man of God, there is death in the pot."

They had found it out in time, and no one seems to have been the worse, but they dare not touch another mouthful. How easy was the remedy. How simple was the answer of the prophet. "Then bring meal." They did so, and he cast it into the deadly soup : and now he said they could take it without fear. "There was no harm in the pot."

Here is a very necessary lesson for "sons of the prophets." The young man was eager to help, was very much in earnest, but in his ignorance he was mixing poison with their food, and it might have caused their death. He thought he was improving the soup, when all the time he was making it quite unfit for food. There are many preachers in the present day who have followed his example. They have gone to the poison vines of German Theology. They have shredded all sorts of errors into their teaching, and "there is death in the pot."

What is to be done ? There is only one remedy. The meal must be added, the pure Word of God. This is the great antidote for the poison of evil doctrine. If we detect the poison flavour of error in anything that is set before us, "then bring meal," and there will be "no harm, no evil thing in the pot."

3. THE POT OF OIL

There is another miracle connected with the sons of the prophets, in which we may find a beautiful hidden picture. One of them had died, but he had died in debt, and his creditors intended to claim the two sons of the dead man and sell them for slaves. The widow came to Elisha in her trouble, told him the story, and said that the creditor had already arrived. What was she to do ?

She had literally nothing in the house but a pot of oil. But this was enough for Elisha. He told her and her sons to go out and borrow from all the neighbours far and near, all sorts of "empty vessels not a few " (2 Kings iv. 3).

The three went from house to house with their strange request. " Can you lend us any empty vessels ? " they said ; and one lent a large pitcher, another two or three small bowls, till at last they had visited every neighbour, and had gathered together as many as they could. The room was quite full—such a strange collection of vessels of all sizes and shapes, alike only in one thing : they were all empty.

And now they were to do as Elisha had said : " Shut the door upon thee and thy sons, and pour out from the pot of oil into all those vessels " ; and each vessel was to be set aside as it was full.   So they shut themselves in the room, and one of the sons brought a vessel to his mother, and she began to fill it.   How eagerly they watched !   It was bigger than their own pot : surely the oil would not fill it ; but as the woman poured, the vessel became fuller and fuller till it reached the brim, and still their own pot was as full as it had ever been !

One son carried the pitcher away and set it by itself, while his brother brought out a second.   This was even larger than the last, but still the oil was sufficient, and so the work went on.   The large vessels were all full, the little bowls and cups were full too, but there was not an empty vessel left, and the oil stayed.

They came out of the room, carefully shutting the door upon their store, and went quickly to the man of God.   " What shall we do now ? " said the widow woman ; and he replied : " Go, sell the oil, and pay the creditor, and live thou and thy children on the rest."

This story reminds us of another miracle

worked through a pot of oil. It took place in the days of Elijah, during the great famine, after the brook Cherith had dried up. When the drought commenced God had told Elijah to go there for He would command the ravens to feed him, and day by day they brought him food. But after a time the brook ran dry, and Elijah was told to go to Sarepta, where God had commanded a widow woman to supply his needs.

Ravens in the one case and a penniless widow in the other seemed very unlikely to be able to provide for the prophet ; but God made no mistake. He showed the ravens where to find the food, and where to deliver it ; and He worked a miracle in the widow's home by which she and her son benefited, as well as Elijah (1 Kings xvii.).

When Elijah arrived at the gate of Sarepta he at once caught sight of the widow collecting sticks. God can always bring people across each other's paths when He wants them to help one another. Elijah asked her first for a drink of water, and as she was going willingly to fetch it, he added a further request : " Bring me, I pray thee, a morsel of bread in thine hand."

She had just come to the end of her re-
sources and was going to make a last little cake
for herself and her son, for she had but "a
handful of meal in a barrel and a little oil in a
cruse." But this was enough! Elijah told
her to make him a little cake first and bring
it to him, and then to make one for herself and
for her son, adding the wonderful promise from
God: "The barrel of meal shall not waste,
neither shall the cruse of oil fail, until the day
that God sendeth rain upon the earth."

The woman obeyed without questioning,
and when she had made the cakes and poured
out some of the oil there was just as much meal
left in the barrel as when she began, and just as
much oil in the cruse. The last time she had
baked bread she had made such a tiny loaf that
there had only been a few mouthfuls for each,
but as she looked into her barrel and found the
meal still undiminished, she felt she need not
stint herself and her boy, and so the loaves
grew larger instead of smaller; and the supply
lasted through the remainder of the three and
a half years of famine.

In order to discover the hidden picture in
these two stories it is well to look at them
together. They are very similar, for they both

have to do with a miraculous supply of oil. Oil throughout the Scriptures is evidently a type of the Holy Spirit, and we learn from these scenes the two great lessons taught by the Lord in the fourth and seventh chapters of John ; though in each of these passages He used the simile of water—another type of the Holy Spirit. In John iv. He spoke to the woman at Sychar's well of a well of water that would spring up in her heart if she came to Him and drank of the water that He would give her. In John vii. He speaks to His disciples, not only of a well in the heart but of overflowing rivers of water.

The woman of Sarepta found the cruse of oil an unfailing supply to meet her need. This was like the well of water of John iv. The widow of one of the sons of the prophets was able to fill from her pot of oil "empty vessels not a few." This was like the rivers of John vii., sufficient to fill other vessels, always overflowing, but never becoming empty by so doing.

Neither the woman of Samaria nor the widow of Sarepta belonged to Israel. The Lord Jesus said : "Many widows were in Israel in the days of Elias, when the heaven was

shut up three years and six months, when great
famine was throughout all the land ; but unto
none of them was Elias sent, save unto Sarepta,
a city of Sidon, unto a woman that was a
widow" (Luke iv. 25, 26). The teaching of
John vii. was specially for the Lord's disciples,
the followers of the greatest Prophet that ever
lived ; while Elisha's miracle, as we have seen,
was connected with the sons of the prophets.

When we come to the Lord as thirsty
sinners, and are satisfied by Him, He gives us
His Holy Spirit to dwell in our heart : "In
whom also, after that ye believed (or upon
believing), ye were sealed with that Holy
Spirit of promise" (Eph. i. 13). "If any man
have not the Spirit of Christ, he is none of
His" (Rom. viii. 9). He shall "abide with
you for ever" (John xiv. 16). This is like
the cruse of oil that wasted not. And if this
well of water continues to spring up unhindered
and unchoked by the things of the world
(comp. Gen. xxvi. 18), there will be overflowing rivers for others. We know that the
Lord, in promising rivers of living water,
referred to the Spirit, for we read : "This
spake He of the Spirit which they that believe
on Him should receive" (John vii. 39). When

He spake the words the Holy Spirit had not been given, for He came down after the Lord's ascension.

The sons of the prophets need to know more and more of this unfailing supply that will fill "empty vessels not a few." It mattered not the size nor the shape, the large ones were filled and the little ones too. The prophet told the woman to sell the oil and pay her debt. It is only as we are filled with the Spirit that we can pay the debts spoken of by the Apostle Paul : "I am debtor both to the Greeks and to the barbarians ; both to the wise and to the unwise." Knowing the Gospel of God concerning the Lord Jesus Christ, he felt that he owed it to his fellowmen to pass on the Good Tidings. We need to be filled with the Spirit in order that we may be able to do this.

Elisha added : "Live thou and thy children on the rest." However much we pass on, we shall still find there is abundance for all our need.

"THOU SHALT SHUT THE DOOR UPON THEE"

If thou too wouldst be blest, then shut thy door ;
Let not the world into thy heart intrude,
Shut out its noise and all its heavy cares.

No curious eyes must see the marvel wrought
When thou dost pray unto thy Father, God,
Who sees in secret, and in secret too,
Delights to give the answer to thy prayer.
Bring forth thy pot of oil and let it flow,
For it is just as rich as that small cruse
From whence the widow poured such wondrous streams.
Bring forth thine empty vessels, fill them all,
And then go forth and let the world be blest.
    Art thou a debtor to the souls around ?
'Tis thus, and thus alone, that thou canst pay.
Go quickly sell thine oil to those without,
For many in the darkness need the light ;
Their lamps untrimmed, are waiting to be filled.
Oh, hoard it not, for soon 'twill be too late,
Too late for thee to sell, for them to buy,
But use the blessing which thou hast received ;
Go pay thy debts and live upon the rest.

THE TALES OF
TWO SIEGES

"Then they said one to another, We do not well: this day is a day of good tidings, and we hold our peace: if we tarry till the morning light some mischief will come upon us: now therefore come, that we may go and tell."

2 Kings 7:9

24

THE TALE OF TWO SIEGES

THE hosts of the Syrians were very powerful in the days of Elisha, but he felt no fear because he had learned, ever since his master Elijah had been caught up, that there was another host far more powerful that was nearer to him than the enemy. The chariots and horses of the heavenly host compassed him round, and when he was besieged in Dothan he knew that they were close beside him, closer than the besieging force.

The king of Syria was specially anxious to capture Elisha, and sent against him "horses and chariots, and a great host; and they came by night and compassed the city about" (2 Kings vi. 14–17). It was no wonder that the servant of Elisha was terrified when he saw such a company, and that he exclaimed: "Alas, my master! How shall we do?" He had not yet learned to say with David: "Though an host should encamp against me, my heart shall not fear" (Psalm xxvii. 3), for he did not know of that other host : " The angel of the Lord encampeth round about them that fear Him, and delivereth them" (Psalm xxxiv. 7). But Elisha knew this, and answered : " Fear not ; for they that be with us are more than they that be with them."

He did not expect his servant merely to take his word for it, but prayed that he might have his eyes opened to see the angel hosts. The prayer was answered, and to his surprise Elisha's servant saw a wonderful sight, for : " Behold, the mountain was full of horses and chariots of fire round about Elisha." What could the Syrians do against such an army ? Again Elisha prayed, and this time it was not for sight for his friend, but that the enemy might be stricken with blindness. Groping in the darkness, they needed someone to guide them ; and, without telling them who he was, Elisha volunteered his services. " I will lead you to the man whom you seek," he said, and he led them to Samaria the capital of the kingdom of Israel.

Then he prayed that their eyes might be opened once more, and, lo, they were in the midst of Samaria, with the Israelites around them, and the man they had been sent to capture standing before them. Elisha would not allow them to be killed or injured ; in those ancient days it was customary for prisoners of war to be treated with courtesy. Elisha said to the king : " Wouldest thou smite those whom thou hast taken captive with thy sword and with thy bow ? " and so at Elisha's direction the king prepared great provision for them : " and when they had eaten and drunk, he sent them away, and they returned to their master."

For some time after this the Syrians came no more into the land of Israel ; but the king had not forgotten his humiliating defeat, and as soon as possible he gathered all his host together and besieged Samaria. The city was very closely shut up, and there was a great famine. The people were in terrible straits, such as had been foretold by God in Deut. xxviii. 52, 53, amongst the evils that would befall the people if they forsook their God and disobeyed His commandments. The siege of Samaria was just such as Moses described, for in the madness of their despair and hunger the people had even killed and eaten their children.

When this came to the ears of the king, he

rent his clothes, but instead of seeing that he and his father Ahab had been the cause of all the evil, he blamed Elisha and determined to take his life. A messenger was sent to arrest the prophet, and the king followed to see that his commands were obeyed ; but before they reached the house, Elisha told the elders who were sitting with him that the messenger was on his way, and that Jehoram the son of Ahab was just behind. Then Elisha made a most astonishing announcement : " To-morrow at this time," he said, " food in abundance will be sold cheaply at the gate of Samaria," and he named the price. It seemed an impossible thing, and one of the courtiers of the king sneered at such a prophecy. " Behold, if the Lord would make windows in heaven might this thing be," he said. Elisha told him that it would surely happen, but though he would see it, he would not eat of the food.

Outside the city were four lepers. According to the law of Moses, their disease obliged them to remain outside the walls, lest others should be defiled ; and there they remained all through the siege, between the Israelites and the Syrians, for the Syrians would certainly not want to take them prisoners. At first their friends within the city managed to supply them with food, but now they had none for themselves, and could not give any to the four lepers.

So on the very day that Elisha had uttered his prophecy they made up their minds to go over to the Syrians. They could not be in a worse condition ; they would certainly die if they remained where they were. In the evening twilight, for they did not want to be seen by the besieged, they arose and crept down to the Syrian camp. But, to their utter amazement, when they reached the tents of the besiegers, they found no trace of a single soldier. What had happened ? They could not tell.

They found in the first tent plenty to eat and drink, and treasures of all sorts, gold and silver and raiment which they eagerly collected ; and when they had hidden their spoil they entered another tent, and found it in the same condition ; no lights were visible save the stars, and they cautiously passed from one tent to another in the darkened camp. Not a sound could they hear of any living creature, man or beast, in the whole encampment.

God himself had come in, and had turned back the invader. He " had made the host of the Syrians to hear a noise of chariots, and a

noise of horses, even the noise of a great host."
The angelic company that had been seen by
Elisha's servant was now heard by the enemy ;
and thinking that relief was coming to the be-
leaguered city, that the kings of the Hittites
and of the Egyptians were close at hand, they
fled for their lives.

The four lepers soon began to realise that
they were acting very selfishly. They remembered that hundreds of people were starving close at hand, and here was plenty for all ;
and so they said one to another : "We do not
well : this day is a day of good tidings and we
hold our peace : if we tarry till the morning
light, some mischief will come upon us : now,
therefore, come that we may go and tell the
king's household " (2 Kings vii. 9).

So in the middle of the night they hurried
back to Samaria, and when they arrived at the
gate they called the porter of the city, and gave
the astonishing news. Although Elisha had
foretold that relief was coming, he had not been
believed, and when the news came it seemed
too good to be true. The king, who had been
awakened from his sleep, immediately arose.
He thought himself very wise, for he quickly
saw as he imagined that it was only a trap.

He explained to his servants that the Syrians knew how hungry they all were, and had merely withdrawn in order to entice them out of the city, and then fall upon them and enter the gates. Any theory was better than believing that God would do as He had said by His servant Elisha.

One of the king's servants, however, suggested that there would be no harm in going to see if the story told by the lepers were true. " Let us send and see." Two poor half-starved horses were saddled, and two of the king's servants rode off to obey the king's command : " Go and see." They soon saw that there was no ambush, the Syrians had really fled, for all the way was strewn with garments and vessels, which they had cast away in their haste. How eagerly the starving Israelites waited the return of the messengers ! And when they heard that the good news was really true, the whole people rushed out and " spoiled the tents of the Syrians."

Flour and barley in abundance were sold at the gate of the city at exactly the price and at exactly the hour predicted by Elisha ; as Mr. Spurgeon once said : " God's Word was fulfilled to the penny and to the hour." The courtier who had sneered at Elisha's words was put in charge of the gate, but the crush of people was so great that it was impossible to keep them back, and he was trodden under foot, and died, having seen the food, but not having eaten of it—just as the prophet had said.

This wonderful story is full of interesting lessons for us. The power of God to deliver is just the same to-day as it was in the days of Elisha, and He could still do just as strange and marvellous things now as then, for : " This God is our God for ever and ever." If only our eyes were opened, we, too, should be able to see the angel hosts encamping around us. " Are they not all ministering spirits, sent forth to minister for them who shall be heirs of salvation ? "

But the chief interest of the story centres in the four lepers. This is where we find the hidden story, for these lepers are just like many of us now. They were in a miserable condition, ready to die, nobody wanted them, no one could help them, and suddenly they found everything that could meet their need.

When their own hunger was appeased, how could they selfishly keep it to themselves ? Is not this a picture of needy sinners who have come to the Lord Jesus, and found unsearchable riches in Him ?   If we have done so, if our heart-hunger has been satisfied, we can say with the lepers when they were keeping it to themselves : " We do not well : this day is a day of good tidings, and we hold our peace . . . now, therefore, come that we may go and tell." How much they had to tell !   It was just what the starving people in Samaria wanted.   How much we have to tell.   It is just what hungry souls all around us need.   It was night-time, and the lepers felt that they must not wait. They said : " If we tarry till the morning light, some mischief will come upon us," or " we shall find punishment " (*marg.*).

We, too, are living in the night season of the Lord's absence.   We are looking for His return, the rising of the Sun that will usher in " the Morning without clouds."   " If we tarry till morning light," it will be too late to tell the starving crowds of the plentiful supply that is to be found in Him.   Our opportunities for publishing the good tidings will be over when we are caught up to meet the Lord in the air. We know that no punishment for our sin will befall us, for the Lord Jesus took the chastisement of our peace upon Himself, and " was wounded for our trangressions," so that

"there is, therefore, now no condemnation
to them which are in Christ Jesus"; yet at
the judgment-seat of Christ we shall "suffer
loss," and receive no approval from Him, if
we have failed to try and win souls for Him.
"Now, therefore, come that we may go and
tell."

THE KING'S SON
SHALL REIGN

"He shewed them the king's son."

2 Kings 11:4b

"He said unto them, Behold, the king's son
shall reign, as the Lord hath said of the sons
of David."

2 Chronicles 23:3b

25

THE KING'S SON SHALL REIGN

FROM the day when "the old serpent" in the garden of Eden heard the words about the Coming One, saying that the Seed of the woman should bruise his head, Satan set himself to destroy that Seed. Many times throughout the Scriptures we can trace his designs. He tried to destroy the seed of Abraham in Egypt, when Pharaoh made the law that all the infants should be killed. He tried it again at Bethlehem, when the infants were slain at the command of Herod.

He nearly succeeded on one occasion, when Athaliah the daughter of Jezebel tried to kill all the "seed royal." The same enemy prompted these three massacres, and in each case the object was the same—in Egypt, in Jerusalem, and in Bethlehem.

Athaliah thought she had succeeded, as Satan must have thought he had succeeded at

Calvary, but on both occasions God thwarted his plot. In spite of Athaliah, "one from among the slain" was taken and hidden in the house of the Lord for six years.

If she had accomplished her purpose, the promises to David would not have been fulfilled ; but God always looks after His own promises. Yet it seemed as though she had succeeded, for "Athaliah did reign over the land." Many in Judah must have been heavy of heart as they saw her power, and believed that she really had "destroyed all the seed royal" (2 Kings xi. 1).

They might have asked : "Where is the promise concerning David's son ? All the power is in the hands of Jezebel's daughter. God said : 'The sceptre shall not depart from Judah until Shiloh come'; and it seems as though it had departed, and Shiloh has not come"; and they were much perplexed.

But one day the faithful in Israel received a private message from the high priest. The elders, the rulers, the Levites, and the captains were summoned to meet Jehoiada, and after entering into a covenant with them, and making them swear allegiance, he told them the wonderful news. "The king's son is still alive.

He has been hidden from you all this time, but he has been quite safe in the house of the Lord. You may be satisfied about one thing : 'Behold the king's son shall reign, as the Lord hath said of the sons of David'" (2 Chron. xxiii. 3). And then "he shewed them the king's son" (2 Kings xi. 4).

What a difference that sight must have made to those who were mourning the reign of the usurper ! With what delight they must have gazed upon the young king ! Life was changed for them from henceforth, and even if they had had to wait a little while for the "crowning day," their hearts would have been at rest. They would have known that it was only for a time, and then the king would come to his own. From the moment they discovered that the rightful heir was alive, they were all on the alert for him to be proclaimed.

After they had had this sight of the king's son, the Levites were given their allotted places, and were stationed as "porters" at the various gates. At the right moment they and the captains of the guard were permitted to enter into the house of the Lord, and were told to compass the king round about. They were gathered round him, so that when he came out

they came out too ; for Jehoiada said to them :
" Be ye with the king when he cometh in, and
when he goeth out."

This scene is one of the most beautiful of
the prophetic pictures of the Old Testament.
The King's Son is still hidden in the house
of the Lord, but " the crowning day is coming
by and by." At Calvary, Satan thought he had
indeed slain the " Seed Royal," but He arose
from the dead, and has been hidden from the
eyes of men for nearly two thousand years.
We know, however, that the god of this world
will not always reign over the land : " The
King's Son shall reign." " He must reign till
He hath put all things under His feet."
Meanwhile there is a secret band of followers
who do not own allegiance to the usurper, for
they have been shown the King's Son. One
glimpse of Him has changed their lives. He
could say : " The world seeth Me no more ; but
ye see Me."

It was just such a discovery that changed
the whole life of Saul of Tarsus. On the road
to Damascus he found out that the One he had
thought to be dead was " alive " (Acts xxv. 19).
" Last of all He was seen of me also " ; and
Saul the persecutor became Paul the Apostle.

During the time of waiting for the crowning day, it is the High Priest that acts. It is from Him that we now receive our orders ; it is He who gives to each his allotted place, who tells us of the blessed hope that is ours. We are waiting to be summoned to take our place by the King's side, when He comes to receive us to Himself. This is His coming *for* His saints. " For the Lord Himself shall descend from heaven with a shout, with the voice of the archangel, and with the trump of God : and the dead in Christ shall rise first : then we which are alive and remain shall be caught up together with them in the clouds to meet the Lord in the air ; and so shall we ever be with the Lord " (1 Thess. iv. 16, 17).

" Till He come " He has " commanded the porter to watch," and all His servants to be ready. " Blessed are those servants whom the Lord when He cometh shall find watching." As the Levites stood expecting the signal, they were provided with spears, bucklers, and shields —not new untried weapons, but those " that had been King David's which were in the house of God." The whole armour of God is given to us, that having done all we too may stand ; and the shield and sword that are pro-

vided are those which were used by our Lord
Himself in His encounters with the enemy.

At last "they brought out the king's son,
and put upon him the crown . . . and made
him king . . . and set the king upon the
throne of the kingdom." This part of the
story represents our Lord's coming *with* His
saints. He who is now the hidden One, who
has only His little band of followers, will one
day be crowned with "many crowns" and then
it will be said : "The kingdoms of this world
are become the kingdoms of our Lord, and of
His Christ : and He shall reign for ever and
ever" (Rev. xi. 15).

But before the king could reign, Athaliah
had to be put to death. "And all the people
of the land rejoiced : and the city was quiet,
after that they had slain Athaliah with the
sword." This is but a faint foreshadowing of
the time when Satan will be bound (Rev. xx.
1, 2), and "the Son of Man shall send forth His
angels, and they shall gather out of His kingdom
all things that offend, and them that do iniquity" (Matt. xiii. 41). As we study this
picture, and hear Him say : "Surely I come
quickly," do not our hearts respond : "Amen.
Even so ; come, Lord Jesus" ?

THE FIERY FURNACE

"When thou walkest through the fire, thou shalt not be burned; neither shall the flame kindle upon thee."

Isaiah 43:2

26

THE FIERY FURNACE

AFTER one of the sieges of Jerusalem, certain young nobles of the seed royal were taken captive by Nebuchadnezzar, and carried away to Babylon. Four of these, probably those of highest rank as well as of most conspicuous faithfulness to God, are well known from the Book of Daniel. He himself was chief of the four, and the others were Hananiah, Mishael, and Azariah. We know them better under their Chaldean names— Shadrach, Meshach, and Abednego. His companions were a great help to Daniel, especially at the beginning of his captivity and exile.

One day they were all in danger of their lives from an edict that had gone forth from Nebuchadnezzar concerning all the wise men. The king had had a remarkable vision which had made a very great impression on him; but when he woke in the morning he could not remember anything of it.   He summoned all the wise men, in the hope that they would be able to tell him the dream and its meaning ; but though they might have invented an interpretation, they could do nothing without being told what the vision itself had been.

The king was very angry at their failure—all these wise men and astrologers, and not one of them could help him ! So in his rage he ordered that they should all be put to death, and Daniel and his three companions were to be slain with the rest.

Arioch, the captain of the king's guard, had already started on his mission. Possibly he had even come to arrest Daniel, but with his usual wisdom and tact Daniel parleyed with him, and suggested that there was no such haste ; he himself would go in unto the king, and ask him that a little time might be granted, and he would then give him the interpretation. Nebuchadnezzar granted his request, for his one desire was to find out what his wonderful vision had been about. If he killed Daniel and the others, he might be destroying all his chances of finding out the secret, and so he told his officers to wait awhile.

Daniel went to his house, and told his three friends about the great danger in which they stood, and they had a little prayer-meeting about it. After they had committed the whole matter to God, and had desired "mercies of the God of heaven," Daniel went to bed and to sleep in perfect peace and confidence ; and we read : "Then was the secret revealed unto Daniel in a night vision."

There was probably no sleep that night for the other wise men in Babylon, but Daniel was not afraid. He did not stay up all night in anxiety and fear, and in his sleep the answer came.

God told him that Nebuchadnezzar had seen a vision of a great image, "whose brightness was excellent, . . . and the form thereof terrible" (Dan. ii. 31). It was made of gold, silver, copper, iron, and clay, and Daniel described exactly what the king had seen in his dream.

Nebuchadnezzar was quite sure that the vision had some great meaning, and Daniel was able to explain that it was indeed so, and to tell him what it meant. It was a representation of the great nations who would rule over the land and nation of

Israel, during the time that they were set aside by God.

It had been God's purpose that the children of Israel should be the greatest world power, as they were in the time of Solomon ; but because of their sin and unbelief, God had taken the power from them and given it to the Gentiles, and first of all to Babylon. "Thou art this head of gold," said Daniel to Nebuchadnezzar, "for the God of heaven hath given thee a kingdom, power, and strength, and glory." The gold would be followed by the silver, the Medes and Persians, who in days to come were to conquer Babylon ; the copper, Greece, would follow, having overcome Persia ; and Greece in its turn would be conquered by the iron, Rome. Some of this vision covers days still future, but probably now near at hand, for Nebuchadnezzar saw a stone fall on the feet of the image and break it to pieces. That stone which is to break in pieces the powers of this world is the Lord Jesus Christ at His coming to set up His kingdom upon earth.

Nebuchadnezzar did not trouble himself about this part of the vision. What interested him was the place that he himself was given in it. He liked being the head of gold, and in the next chapter (Dan. iii.) we read that, remembering his vision, he had a gigantic image of gold made, and set up on a plain in a suburb of the city of Babylon. When it was finished, all the princes, governors, and officials in the land, and all the chief of the people were gathered together for the great ceremony of its dedication.

A herald went forth and proclaimed that all the people, whatever their nationality and language, directly they heard the music begin were to fall down and worship "the golden image that Nebuchadnezzar the king had set up." Anyone who refused to do so was to be immediately cast into a burning fiery furnace. But, whilst the crowds were prostrate on their faces, Shadrach, Meshach, and Abednego, who had been set over the affairs of the provinces at Babylon, stood erect, and refused to worship the big idol. The news that they would not do so was soon carried to the king, who was filled with rage and fury, and commanded that the three Jewish princes should at once be cast into the furnace, which was to be made seven times hotter than usual.

The three faithful followers of Jehovah, tightly bound with ropes, were taken up

and cast into the midst of the furnace, and
so terrific was the heat that poured forth from
the mouth of the furnace that the mighty men
who executed the sentence were slain. As
Nebuchadnezzar watched to see what would
happen, to his amazement he saw his three
victims rise to their feet, unbound, for the fire
had done them no harm, and had merely burned
away the ropes. But there was something still
more marvellous, he saw that they had a companion in the furnace ; there was a fourth with
them, and "the form of the fourth is like the
Son of God."

Then Nebuchadnezzar could stand it no
longer. He went as near as he dared to the
mouth of the fiery furnace and called Shadrach,
Meshach, and Abednego by name, and bade
them come forth. "Come hither," he said,
and they obeyed without any difficulty. But he
did not ask the fourth, the One like the Son of
God, to accompany them. Surely it would
have made a great difference to his own history
and the history of Babylon if he had done so.

This story of such thrilling interest is a
beautiful illustration of the exhortation of
the Apostle Paul : "I beseech you therefore,
brethren, by the mercies of God, that ye

present your bodies a living sacrifice, holy, acceptable unto God, which is your reasonable service. And be not conformed to this world ; but be ye transformed by the renewing of your mind, that ye may prove what is that good, and acceptable, and perfect, will of God."

Nebuchadnezzar, when they had come forth unharmed, blessed "the God of Shadrach, Meshach, and Abednego who . . . delivered His servants that trusted in Him . . . and yielded their bodies, that they might not serve or worship any god except their own God" (Dan. iii. 28). They refused to be "conformed to this world," and presented their "bodies a living sacrifice." They considered it "their reasonable service," for they knew that "Our God whom we serve is able to deliver us" (v. 17). And so when they were cast into the fiery furnace they were "transformed," their bonds were burned, and they were freed. "Through faith" they "quenched the violence of fire" (Heb. xi. 34), so that it had no power over them ; and they had no hurt, "nor was an hair of their head singed, neither were their coats changed, nor the smell of fire had passed on them."

A miracle was performed in answer to their

faith, and, better still, they had the presence with them in the fire of the One who was not only like the Son of God, but who was the Son of God Himself. He had promised : "When thou walkest through the fire, thou shalt not be burned ; neither shall the flame kindle upon thee" (Isa. xliii. 2). This was literally fulfilled, and thus they proved "the good and acceptable will of God" as all do who present their bodies thus.

The trial through which they had passed had not even singed their clothes, but it had been a wonderful testimony to the power of Jehovah ; and even Nebuchadnezzar had to confess that "there is no other god that can deliver after this sort." The actual furnace is but a picture of the fiery trials through which God sometimes allows His children to pass. But they too will be delivered, they too have the Lord's presence with them, and if others who watch them can see that He is walking with them in the fire, what glory it will bring to His name. This wonderful scene was probably one link in the chain that at last brought the mighty monarch, Nebuchadnezzar, truly to "praise and extol and honour the King of heaven" (Dan. iv. 37).

THE GOLDEN SCEPTRE

"The king held out to Esther the golden sceptre that was in his hand. So Esther drew near and touched the top of the sceptre."

Esther 5:2b

27

THE GOLDEN SCEPTRE

WE have already discovered one hidden picture in the story of a queen—the Queen of Sheba — who appeared before a king—Solomon—with her questions and her petitions ; but there is another royal interview from which we may learn a beautiful lesson.

Esther was a lovely Jewish maiden who was amongst the exiles in a far country, one of the children of the captivity. She was an orphan, for her parents had evidently died soon after they had been carried away into Babylon, and she had been brought up by her uncle, Mordecai. Ahasuerus, the mighty king of the Medes and Persians, had given orders that all the most beautiful maidens should be brought before him, that he might choose one of them as a bride for himself, and out of all the number his choice fell upon Esther. "The king loved Esther above all the women, and she obtained grace and favour in his sight more than all the virgins ; so that he set the royal crown upon her head and made her queen instead of Vashti " (Esther ii. 17).

The Jews had a very powerful enemy called Haman, who was specially jealous of Mordecai, and so he plotted to destroy all the Jews in the lands ruled by Ahasuerus. It had not become known that Esther was a Jewess, and so Mordecai came to tell her of the danger in which they all stood, and begged her to go in to the king and petition him on their behalf. The Eastern potentate was not easy of approach. "Whosoever . . . shall come unto the king into the inner court, who is not called, there is one law of his to put him to death." But an exception was made for any "to whom the king shall hold out the golden sceptre " (Esther iv. 11).

Esther was very much afraid of going in before the king, but her love for her people, and her desire to obey Mordecai made her determine to venture. She put on her royal apparel, and stood in the inner court within sight of the throne upon which the king was sitting. And "when the king saw Esther the queen standing in the court, she obtained favour in his sight ; and the king held out to Esther the golden sceptre that was in his hand. So Esther drew near and touched the top of his sceptre." The king did not blame her for coming, but said : " What wilt thou, Queen Esther ? And what is thy request ? It shall be even given thee to the half of the kingdom."

The story of the Queen of Sheba coming to Solomon is a beautiful type of the sinner coming to the Lord Jesus. She was a stranger coming to one whom she had never seen. But here we have a picture of one who is already united to the king, who has been lifted to a place by his side, and she is seen bringing her request. This illustrates the Lord's teaching about prayer in John xiv.–xvi. ; for in these wonderful parting words the King is promising always to hold out His golden sceptre. We hear Him saying again and again to all His own : " Whatsoever ye shall ask in My name, that will I do."

None might approach the Eastern monarch but those who had been called. We have been called into our Lord's presence. He says : " Let Me see thy countenance, let Me hear thy voice ; for sweet is thy voice, and thy countenance is comely." And so we may "come boldly to the throne of grace."

It is the blood of the Lamb that makes this possible ; and thus we are brought to the point from which we started in the first of the hidden pictures. It will be noticed that there is great " progress of doctrine " in these Old Testament stories. They begin with the simplest truths for the unsaved, and end with deepest teaching for even experienced Christians. The story of Abel's Lamb tells us of God's " whosoever " for the sinner, for "whosoever will" may come. The story of Esther and the golden sceptre speaks to us of His " whatsoever " for His own children. "Whatsoever ye shall ask in My name that will I do." "And if we know that He hear us, whatsoever we ask, we know that we have the petitions that we desired of Him."

If we have been accepted because of the blood of the Lamb, let us not be afraid to come often into the King's presence with our requests. Esther's petition was not for herself, but for her people, and we too may touch the golden sceptre on behalf of others. "Ask, and ye shall receive, that your joy may be full."

INDEX